STAMP LOVERS NOW HAVE A BOOK to treasure along with their prized collections. *Treasury of Stamps* is everything a work of its kind should be: a superbly illustrated panorama of stamps, a thorough analysis of stamp design and printing, and a complete history of postal services. David Lidman, the author, was for many years Stamps Editor of the *New York Times*. H. Landshoff, whose superb photographs illustrate two other best-selling Abrams books, *The Shell* and *The Doll*, is responsible for the illustrations.

Postage stamps are, as the author points out, one in the series of steps in the history of human communications that lead from the clay tablets of the ancient Near Eastern civilizations to the airmail and even moon mail of today. As background to the story of the postage stamp, Mr. Lidman focuses on some of the unusual ways in which man has sent messages, including the runners of ancient Greece and Persia, the extraordinary private postal service established and maintained for three centuries by the German Princes of Thurn und Taxis, the early "special delivery" systems of Renaissance Italy, the knotted-string contrivances (*quipus*) of the Andean civilization, the royal couriers of England, and the Pony Express in the United States. The first true postage stamps—the famous Penny Black and Two Pence Blue—were issued by England in 1840 during the reign of Queen Victoria.

Arresting as the historical survey is, the real beauty of this volume lies in its treatment of the actual stamps. The author sees them as a reflection of their times, as the products of an exacting craft, and as an exquisite art form. He supports his view by examining every facet of stamp design and printing. The making of an art object within the strict confines of this form has intrigued some of the most successful artists, and perhaps the most compelling section of the book consists of replies to the question "What is good stamp design?" which was put to some of the world's ranking stamp designers.

The final chapter, "Collectors, Stamps, and Philately," dwells entertainingly on stamp lovers as a group. Colorful anecdotes about such collectors as George V of England, Franklin D. Roosevelt, piano king Theodore Steinway, and Francis Cardinal Spellman let the reader know he is in good company.

Following the text, hundreds of stamps are reproduced in large size, arranged by subject. Nothing pertaining to man and his world is missing—the animal kingdom, art and architecture, business and industry, government and politics, literature and music, science, sports, war and peace, and natural phenomena—all fields are represented, along with portraits of their outstanding personalities. A selection of American Bicentennial commemorative issues is included with this volume in a special portfolio. *Treasury of Stamps*, with its lavish illustrations (most in full color) will kindle or recharge an enthusiasm for stamps in anyone who even glances through it.

TREASURY OF STAMPS

1,200 RARE AND BEAUTIFUL STAMPS IN COLOR

TREASURY OF STAMPS

TEXT BY
DAVID LIDMAN

PHOTOGRAPHS BY
H. LANDSHOFF

HARRY N. ABRAMS, INC., PUBLISHERS, NEW YORK

The stamps in the volume are enlarged in varying degrees, conforming with federal regulations governing reproduction of postage stamps in color.

Library of Congress Cataloging in Publication Data

Lidman, David.
    Treasury of stamps.

    Bibliography: p.
    Includes index.
    1. Postage-stamps. 2. Postage-stamps—Collectors
and collecting. I. Title.
HE6182.L52   769'.56   74–32120
ISBN 0-8109-0469-1

Library of Congress Catalogue Card Number: 74–32120
Published by Harry N. Abrams, Incorporated, New York, 1975
All rights reserved. No part of the contents of this book may be
reproduced without the written permission of the publishers
Printed and bound in Japan

Contents

A Collection of Rare and Beautiful Stamps

Preface and Acknowledgments

THE PURPOSE OF THIS BOOK is twofold: to give a brief history of postal service as it developed after man learned to write and to illustrate by-products of the post, some of the nearly 200,000 postage stamps that have appeared since 1840, when an engraved portrait of the youthful Queen Victoria graced the first stamp ever issued. Not all facets of the history of postal service are discussed in the text, but some of the more arresting phases of its development and links with historical events and a few of the interesting people involved are described.

The illustrations include a number of the stamps that collectors refer to as "Classics," stamps, mostly handsome monochromes, that appeared early in the history of stamp emissions. These were usually engraved, occasionally lithographed. Other illustrations show modern stamps produced by the photographic techniques and high-speed multicolor presses that have been instrumental in the outpouring of postage stamps in recent years.

I hope this book will stimulate the reader to become a member of the community of stamp collectors, joining millions around the world who will be happy to make room for many more in the joy of collecting and studying these colorful bits of paper.

While only two names appear as creators of this book, that of the author of the text and the man who photographed almost all of the 1,200 or more illustrations in the volume, acknowledgments are due to many people, including the authors of numerous articles clipped over the years from journals and many associates who have added to the author's knowledge. In both instances it would be foolhardy to attempt to name everyone, but the author's appreciation and gratitude are expressed herewith.

A few people have gone beyond friendship and long association in making possible some aspects of the book:

Special thanks are extended to Jacques Minkus of Gimbels Stamp Departments and Minkus Publications, Inc., New York; to Sheldon Paris, George Tlamsa, and Ben Blumenthal of his executive and editorial staffs; and especially to Mrs. Gloria Wong and Mrs. Estelle Mudayh, who patiently and painstakingly supplied almost all the twentieth-century postage stamps illustrated herein. Without their constant assistance for more than two years, this book would not have been possible.

Others who were of great help include Mrs. Nancie Wall (Mrs. David Rabe) and Frank L. Sente, formerly librarians at the American Philatelic Research Library, State College, Pa.; Mrs. Josephine Eldridge, Mrs. Anne Pritchard, of the staff, and Ernest C. Wilkens, chairman of the library committee, the Collectors Club, New York; A. G. Rigo de Righi, curator, National Philatelic Museum, London; Arthur Salm of Chicago; A. Siegel and Theodore Behr of Robert A. Siegel Auctions, Inc., New York; Bernard D. Harmer, H. R. Harmer, Inc., International Stamp Auctioneers, New York; S. P. Wang, Director General of Posts, Republic of China, Formosa; Raymond H. and Roger G. Weill, Raymond H. Weill Co., New Orleans; Leon Norman and Maurice Williams, London; Belmont Faries of the *Washington Star-News*; Frank Molloy and Jack Wiggins of the *New York Times*.

I am grateful to Richard M. Graf, professor of French and Education at Kingsborough Community College of the City University of New York, for his translation of the poem by Jean Loret.

I wish to express my thanks to the designers who participated in the symposium "What Is Good Stamp Design?"

I owe a special debt of gratitude to Herman Landshoff, the patient photographer who made the color transparencies from which more than 1,000 of the illustrations were produced. Among the staff of Harry N. Abrams, Inc., I want to extend my thanks to Lisa Pontell and Deirdre Silberstein, who organized a vast amount of photographic material, to Dirk Luykx, who arranged it all into an attractive and imaginative design, and to my diligent editor, Patricia Gilchrest.

My warm thanks are extended to the many others, listed below, who have assisted me with illustrative material or research.

David J. Baker, Indianapolis; Russell Bennett, Editor, Stanley Gibbons Magazines, London; George Blizil, Editor, *German Postal Specialist*, Hollywood, Florida; Herbert J. Bloch, Mercury Stamp Co., New York; Robert B. Brandeberry, Wilmington, Del.; George W. Brett, Spirit Lake, Iowa; James A. Conlon, Director, Bureau of Engraving and Printing, Washington, D.C.; P. J. Drossos, Athens; Mrs. Lois Evans, Brookline, Mass.; Dr. Maurice R. Friend, New York; Louis Grunin, Spring Valley, N.Y.

Marc Haas, New York; R. F. York, director, Harrison & Sons, High Wycombe, England; Creighton C. Hart, Kansas City, Mo.; Arlene B. Hirschfelder, Association on American Indian Affairs, Inc., New York; Dr. Soichi Ichida, Tokyo; Ryohei Ishikawa, Tokyo; Morton Dean Joyce, New York; Wallace W. Knox, Oakland, Calif.; Harry Mark, Indianapolis; A. L. Michael, Stanley Gibbons, Ltd., London; Melvin R. Nathan, San Rafael, Calif.; Emilio Obregon, Mexico City.

Per Paag, Arne Almquist, and Carl-Filip Borgh, General Directorate of Posts, Stockholm; Col. John F. Rider, New York; Anthony C. Russo, Chicago; Stampazine, New York; Donald W. Smith, Europa Study Unit, American Topical Association; the United Nations Postal Administration, Ole Hamann, chief, Ivo Lovincic, and Ludo Sturc; the United States Postal Service, Gordon Morison, director, Office of Stamps, Jack Williams, and Herbert Harris; Theo Van Damm, Brewster, N.Y.; Irwin R. Weinberg, Wilkes-Barre, Pa.; Fred S. Wolfe, San Francisco, Calif.

DAVID LIDMAN

11

TREASURY OF STAMPS

1, 2. Egyptian hieroglyphics and an Assyrian tablet are shown on these Austrian stamps designed by Otto Stefferl for WIPA, an international stamp show held in Vienna in 1965.

1

2

THE WORLD'S FIRST POSTAGE STAMPS, the British Penny Black and Two Pence Blue, both bearing the beautifully engraved portrait of Queen Victoria, were issued on May 6, 1840. Although stamps have since been produced in various forms and sizes, their basic appearance today remains very much that of the first: bits of paper about an inch wide and slightly longer with a glutinous wash on the back. Adhesive stamps immediately increased the use of the mails, for they made the post both cheaper and speedier, but when the postage stamp was invented, the communication of messages by the written word had already been known to the world for a very long time. Once man began to write, the mails began.

Men have communicated with each other in many ways, including hand signs, bonfires, drums, shouts from high places, notched sticks, and knotted cords. Symbols conveying an entire message have been exchanged: the olive branch indicating a desire for peace is a well-known example. There have been couriers who memorized messages. None of these systems has ever equaled the written word for accuracy and confidentiality. Centuries ago, the written word in the form of a letter became the surest means of communication for men separated by distance.

The remotest ancestor of handwriting is probably the picture shorthand of the Sumerians, which originated about five thousand years ago in Mesopotamia. The Sumerians developed an alphabet of sorts from "pictographs," little drawings in the sand or on cave walls devised to transmit a message or a thought. From the pictographs came wedge-shaped symbols that eventually evolved into an alphabet. About 3500 B.C. the Egyptians independently developed their hieroglyphics.

"Neither snow, nor rain..."

3–5. Iranian issues of 1973 showing tablets with cuneiform writing.

Using an alphabet or hieroglyphics, messages could be written on clay tablets and sent by a messenger on foot or on horseback. Verbal messages, however, as any reading of the classical historians shows, by no means vanished: couriers continued for centuries to carry the news in their heads.

Most messages, whether verbal or written on clay tablets, were sent and received by rulers, but in some parts of the ancient world tablets that are business records of merchants survive, showing that there was commercial correspondence as well. Notable finds of such mercantile records have been made in the region that is now central Turkey, called Cappadocia in ancient times.

The letter writer of the ancient Middle East was many centuries ahead of his time in one respect: he already had envelopes. The Cappadocian correspondent, after baking his clay tablet, which was about the size of the old-fashioned bean bag, prevented the message from being read by the bearer or other unauthorized eyes by encasing the tablet in a clay wrapper. He then wrote the address on it with a sharp-pointed bit of wood, metal, or bone, and baked the whole once more in an oven. Upon its delivery, the recipient tapped the letter on a hard object, and the outer wrapper broke apart, revealing the message.

The earliest well-developed system of communications belonged to the mighty Persian empire of the sixth and fifth centuries B.C. The Persians had a good system of roads, which were used primarily by couriers on horseback carrying messages for the king. In recounting the wars of the Greeks and Persians, the Greek traveler and historian Herodotus described how the Persian king Xerxes transmitted to his capital the story of his defeat by the Greeks at the battle of Salamis in 480 B.C. Herodotus wrote:

> Xerxes . . . sent off a messenger to carry intelligence of his misfortune to Persia. . . . Nothing mortal travels so fast as these Persian messengers. The entire plan is a Persian invention; and this is the method of it. Along the whole line of road there are men (they say) stationed with horses, in number equal to the number of days which the journey takes, allowing a man and horse to each day; and these men will not be hindered from accomplishing at their best speed the distance which they have to go, either by snow, or rain, or heat, or by the darkness of night. The first rider delivers his despatch to the second, and the second passes it to the third; and so it is borne from hand to hand along the whole line, like the light in the torch-race, which the Greeks celebrate to Vulcan. The Persians give the riding post in this manner, the name of *angarum*.

One line of this description has become familiar to millions of Ameri-

6. A letter of c. 2100 B.C., a tablet wrapped in an envelope of clay. Sumerian (?).

7. The face of a letter tablet, c. 2100 B.C. Sumerian (?).

8. An Athens cancel marking the Allied victory in 1945, commemorated here by the Marathon hero, Pheidippides.

cans because in slightly different form it is chiseled over the entrance of the General Post Office of New York City. When that building was under construction on Eighth Avenue between Thirty-first and Thirty-third streets in 1910–13, the architect, William M. Kendall, cast about for an apt quotation to place above the doors. He found this description by Herodotus, but was dissatisfied with the rhythm of the George Rawlinson translation given above. Himself the son of a teacher of classical languages, Kendall reworked the sentence to read: "Neither snow, nor rain, nor heat, nor gloom of night stays these couriers from the swift completion of their appointed rounds," and in that form it was placed over the Post Office doors. As many guide books have pointed out, this is probably the longest inscription on any public building in the United States.

Post stations were established in the Persian Empire at the distance a horse could travel in a day, the way stations ("excellent caravansaries," according to Herodotus) providing rest facilities as well as fresh horses for couriers in the king's service.

When the writers of the Old Testament mention "posts," it is usually this Persian system of which they are speaking. About the seventh century B.C., the author of the book of Jeremiah, in prophesying the fall of Jerusalem to the Babylonians (which came about in 586 B.C.), wrote: "One post shall run to meet another, and one messenger to meet another, to show the king of Babylon that his city is taken at one end" (51:31). The unhappy Job wrote: "Now my days are swifter than a post: they flee away, they see no good" (9:25).

Everyday people could not be said to participate in this system of posts. It was used either by commercial enterprise, as shown by the merchants' letters of Cappadocia, or by royalty. Only a few people were literate anyway. Ordinary people still relied on traveling friends to transmit verbal messages to distant acquaintances.

In Greece there were messenger services between the city-states, at least in the infrequent times of peace, and roads for the use of couriers, who were usually on foot. It was during the Persian Wars that the most famous exploit of a Grecian runner occurred. According to Herodotus (Book 6. 105–6) a runner named Phidippides was sent to request military help from the city of Sparta before the battle of Marathon (490 B.C.). The distance, which is 150 miles, was normally a four-day run, but Phidippides covered it in two. After the Greeks had beaten the more numerous Persians at Marathon, it was the same Phidippides who ran the twenty-six miles from Marathon to the *agora* (town square) of Athens and shouted *"Nike"* ("Victory!") to the citizens. He then, as legend has it, dropped dead. Today's modern marathon, an Olympic event, a long-distance running race 26 miles, 385 yards in length, is a memorial to Phidippides.

18

Egyptian civilization, so advanced in so many ways, did not fail to develop a messenger service. By 2000 B.C. there was an efficient system of couriers for Egypt's rulers and merchants. The main settlements along the Nile were linked by roads to the inland settlements and military outposts. Horses were introduced into Egypt by the nomadic Hyksos people, who conquered the country about 1675 B.C., and the couriers then became horsemen.

CLAY TO PAPYRUS TO PARCHMENT

Messages and letters were written first on clay tablets, then on papyrus, then on parchment (the skin of animals), and eventually, thanks to the Chinese, on paper. An extraordinarily versatile Nile plant played a major role in the development of writing. The papyrus *(Cyperus papyrus)* had many uses for the ancient Egyptians: its roots were burned as fuel; the pith was eaten; the stems, which were flexible, were woven into

9. Portion of a letter written in Greek on papyrus. From Egypt, c. A.D. 162.

twine, sandals, boats and their sails, baskets, and so on. But for the history of human communication, the important fact about the papyrus plant was that it could be formed into sheets by laying longitudinal slices side by side in two layers at right angles and pressing them together with an adhesive made by mixing the juice of the plant with Nile water. The sheets were glued end to end and rolled to form a manuscript, also called papyrus. This invention by unknown hands and at an unknown date was of great consequence in the history of writing because it produced a surface for receiving writing which was far superior to the clay tablets. On papyrus entire books could be written.

Parchment is said to derive its name from the ancient city of Pergamum in Asia Minor, which is now Bergama in western Turkey. In the last centuries before Christ, the rulers of the city, a center of culture, built up a library of books written on this substance. Parchment, or vellum, is produced by soaking and rubbing the skins of sheep, goats, or cattle until there is a surface smooth enough to take ink. Parchment is more durable than papyrus. An extra advantage of parchment was that unlike papyrus, which had to be used in the form of a scroll, it could be stitched into volumes called codices. Any attempt to stitch papyrus broke the fibers and made it brittle.

The Chinese are said to have invented paper in A.D. 105. In the paper-making process vegetable fibers were reduced to pulp into which a mold was dipped. The fibers were then shaken in the mold to cross them for strength and turned out onto a cloth. The water was repeatedly pressed out, and the sheets, now paper, were dried. The same basic technique is still used.

The spread of paper as a writing substance was very slow. The first European country in which it was used was probably Spain, where the Moors are believed to have introduced it in the twelfth century. Mills were established in other parts of Europe in the next three centuries, but the pace was sluggish. There was not a paper mill in England, for example, until 1495. Parchment continued to be used for centuries and indeed is sometimes used today.

THE ROMAN WAY

By far the most extensive and most efficient road and messenger system in the ancient world was that established by the Romans in their empire. The system of roads and posts was called the *cursus publicus,* but the modern reader should not be misled by this name: the *cursus publicus* was by no means a public post open to all comers, as the name might imply. It was primarily conducted by the government for the government's use. Nevertheless, the magnitude of the Roman mail operation was awesome. The historian Edward Gibbon noted that

> the great chain of communication . . . was drawn out to the length of four thousand and eighty Roman miles . . . [the roads] ran in a direct line from one city to another, with very little respect for the obstacles either of nature or private property. Mountains were perforated, and bold arches thrown over the broadest and most rapid streams. . . . Houses were everywhere erected at a distance only of five or six miles; each of them was constantly provided with forty horses, and by the help of these relays it was easy to travel 100 miles a day along the Roman roads. The use of the posts was allowed to those who claimed it by an Imperial mandate; but though originally intended for the public service, it was sometimes indulged to the business or conveniency of private citizens.

The roads were primarily military highways for the dispatch of troops, but they were also used by mounted messengers. Distances were marked by stones at each Roman mile, approximately 1,620 yards. Among the first Roman roads to be constructed was the celebrated Appian Way, traditionally begun in 312 B.C. by order of Appius Claudius the Censor.

THE CALIPHS

Among the states that succeeded the Roman Empire, one of the most important in terms of communications was the empire of the Arabs. During the flowering of Mohammedan culture in the seventh and eighth centuries A.D. a communications network was laid out across the Near East and northern Africa on the pattern established earlier by the Persians.

One of the great caliphs of the eighth century, Abu Jafar Mansur, wrote, "My throne rests on four pillars and my power on four men: a blameless judge, an energetic chief of police, an honest minister of finance, and a faithful postmaster, who gives me reliable information on everything."

From the capital at Baghdad six main roads spread out over the Arab domains with 930 post stations functioning in the ninth century. The postmasters also acted as intelligence agents, gathering information and passing it on to the central authorities.

CHINA

The postal system in China is extremely ancient. Horse posts operated by the central government are known to have existed about a thousand

10, 11. These two strips of five stamps issued by the Republic of China in 1972 were adapted from portions of unsigned watercolor-and-ink silk scrolls of the Ming Dynasty (1368–1644) in the National Palace Museum, Taipei, Taiwan (Formosa). The scrolls, 3.2 feet high and 85.9 feet and 98.2 feet long, respectively, depict a round-trip journey from Peking to the imperial tombs at Cheng-tien undertaken by the twelfth Ming emperor, Shih-tsung (1522–1566). The Departure flow, from right to left, by land; the Return, from left to right, by water. The emperor, slightly larger than the other figures, is on horseback to the left of the first vertical perforations.

12. A Japanese stamp of 1940, depicting the legendary sacred Golden Kite which perched on the bow of Japan's first emperor, Jimmu Tenno, emanating a dazzling light that blinded his foes, enabling him to achieve the victory that solidified his empire.

years before Christ, during the reign of the Western Chou dynasty.

The founder of the Han dynasty, which reigned from 202 B.C. to A.D. 220, is said to be a man by that name who began his career in officialdom as a postmaster. The best account received by the Western world of the Chinese posts during the Middle Ages came of course from the fluent pen of the Venetian Marco Polo, who spent the years 1275–92 in the China ruled by Kublai Khan. Polo wrote:

> You must know that the city of Khan-balik [Peking] is a center from which many roads radiate to many provinces, one to each. . . . The whole system is admirably contrived. When one of the Great Khan's messengers sets out along any of these roads he has only to go twenty-five miles, and there he finds a posting station. . . . At every post the messengers find a spacious and palatial hostelry for their lodging . . . splendid beds with rich coverlets of silk and all that befits an emissary of high rank. If a king came here, he would be well lodged. Here the messengers find no less than 400 horses. . . . Posts such as these at distances of twenty-five or thirty miles are to be found along all the main highways. . . . When the messengers are traveling . . . where there are no homesteads or habitation, they find . . . posts with the same palatial accommodations and the same supply of horses. . . . This is surely the highest privilege and the greatest resource ever enjoyed by man on earth. . . . The whole organization is so stupendous and so costly that it baffles speech and writing.

Unmounted couriers, Polo wrote, "wear large belts hung all around with bells so that when they run they are audible at a great distance. They always run at full speed and never for more than three miles. And at the next station, three miles away, where the noise they make gives due notice of their approach, another courier is waiting." Polo then asserts that "I can assure you that by means of that service of unmounted couriers, the Great Khan receives news over a ten days journey in a day and a night." The relay-running couriers also supported the mounted messengers at night, running ahead of the messengers with lighted lanterns.

As in the Near East and Europe, these ancient posts were intended for the royal couriers; private citizens had no access to these services.

It was not until the fifteenth century that private letter posts were created in China. The "law of avoidance," by which, to prevent fraud, government officials were forbidden to serve in their native provinces, dates from that time. These officials, assigned to distant provinces and wishing to communicate with their homes, employed private letter companies to send mail. This type of service lasted until modern times.

Railroads were not built in China until late in the nineteenth century, and during China's decadence communications became slow and unreliable. The earliest postage stamps of China were not issued until 1878. Even then, they were not produced by the government. They were issued by the Imperial Maritime Customs Post, which was directed by Sir Robert Hart, a remarkable Englishman who spent most of his life in China. He was given the job of establishing an up-to-date postal service, and in it used the people he had trained in the customs houses.

Foreign post offices run by alien governments existed in China until the 1920s. They were established by the governments of Japan, Russia, Great Britain, France, Italy, Germany, and the United States under various treaties with the Chinese government. They operated in China's ports under the direction of the consulates of the various countries, handling mail for their nationals and others who might have letters going to the home country. They generally used the stamps of their own nation overprinted for the offices in China.

In Japan rudimentary courier routes existed for at least twelve hundred years before the country was opened to the West in the 1860s. Soon after contact with the U.S. and Europe began, a British envoy commented that Japan was three centuries behind the rest of the civilized world in all that concerned communication. The post had no reference to the wants of the people but served merely for governmental messages. A courier carried his sealed letter stretched out before him in a cleft bamboo stick, and, following the custom in China, wore a little tinkling bell to announce his appearance. In a short time, however, beginning in 1868, improvements were made in the post under S. M. Bryan, an American adviser who set up a system based on that of the U.S., including the issuance of the first Japanese stamps in 1871. Today, the Japanese postal system is considered one of the world's best.

13. Japanese stamp of 1960, commemorating the centenary of the United States–Japan Treaty of Amity and Commerce. Designed by Gyo Fujikawa.

14. Colorful costumes of regional Thurn und Taxis postal officials of the principality of Reuss, 1847.

Thurn und Taxis: The Family Postal Union

A PRIVATE ENTERPRISE provided the best-organized postal service in Europe for the first four centuries of the modern era. From about 1450 to 1867, mail routes covering much of the continent were established and conducted by a single family of the high nobility of the Holy Roman Empire—the house of Thurn und Taxis. Serving at first only rulers and officials, the Thurn und Taxis mails eventually were opened to anyone who wanted to send a letter. This remarkably long-lived family business was a major force in bettering communication by post.

Thurn und Taxis is the Germanization of a name that was originally Italian—Della Torre e Tasso. The Della Torre family were briefly lords of the city-state of Milan in the thirteenth century and took their name from the tower fortress that was their stronghold. They were expelled from Milan in 1277 by their rivals, the Visconti family, who were also to have a place in postal history (see page 12). The Della Torre took refuge at Monte Tasso near the city of Bergamo, north of Milan, and soon added Tasso (which means badger) to their family name. Their coat of arms depicted the origins of that name, displaying both a tower and a badger. After the family entered the mail business, it became customary for their messengers to place the pelt of a badger across the foreheads of their post horses.

The Della Torre e Tasso established a service for the delivery of letters first in Italy with the Compagna dei Corieri Bergamashi (The Bergamascan Company of Messengers), and then in Germany, when in 1450 Roger Della Torre e Tasso became postmaster of Frederick III, the Holy Roman Emperor, and organized a postal service for the imperial possessions in central Europe. In 1516 the emperor Maximilian I granted

25

Egenwärtige ESTAFFETTA soll unverzüglich bey Tag und Nacht nacher *Rehda* geführt/ und nirgends keines wegs im wenigsten auffgehalten/ verhindert/ noch versaumet werden/ dann Ihrer Römischen Käyserlichen Majeſt. Unserm Allergnädigsten Herrn auch allen Chur-Fürsten und Ständen des Heil. Röm. Reichs viel daran gelegen/ und sollen alle Posthalter den Tag und Stundt des Empfangs und Abfertigung fleißig hierunter verzeichnen. Signatum Paderborn den 12 april. 1757.

Abgangen umb 10½ Uhr

Der Röm. Käyſ. Majeſt.
Postmeister.

15

PASS-
und
STAFFETTEN-Zettul
von Paderborn
nach

Rehda

Cito
Cito
Citissimé

16

Beylage zu No. 207.
der Frankfurter Kaiserl. Reichs-Ober-Post-Amts-Zeitung.

Donnerstag, den 28. December 1797.

17

15, 16. Official pass of Thurn und Taxis postmen, for use between Paderborn and Rehda, 1757. Postmen were required to travel a specified distance in a specified time, and their passage time had to be certified by postmasters. Carriers were docked for every fifteen minutes they were tardy. *Cito* means "hasten."

17. Supplement No. 207 of the newspaper of the main post office of Thurn und Taxis at Frankfurt, December 28, 1797.

18. The "Ladies" cover of the Thurn und Taxis posts, c. 1852.

to Francesco Della Torre e Tasso, Roger's son, the imperial privilege of maintaining postal routes from Vienna to Brussels, Brussels to France and Spain, and Vienna to the Italian states. Francesco's descendants increased the routes and attempted to gain a monopoly of all postal service in the empire. From 1615 they were hereditary imperial postmasters general, and they were also ennobled under the name Thurn und Taxis, advancing in rank until in 1695 they were created princes of the Holy Roman Empire.

Among the more than three hundred states of the empire there was marked opposition to the continuing—and highly profitable—expansion of the Thurn und Taxis mail routes. A few states (notably Brandenburg-Prussia) persisted in operating their own posts, but generally the imperial privilege kept the couriers of Thurn und Taxis—traveling by foot, horse, or coach, and by both main roads and bypaths—serving the rulers of Europe. When, in the early years of the sixteenth century, the imperial

19. A dispatch from the Holy Roman Emperor Ferdinand I to his chancellor and councillors of Lower Austria, signed by the emperor, 1556.

20. A cover of a letter from Lamoral de Thurn und Taxis at Brussels to his Cologne postmaster, 1675.

21. Thurn und Taxis postal routes in the early sixteenth century.

treasury was unable to pay the annual stipend, the couriers were permitted to carry mail for ordinary citizens, charging fixed fees. This was the first true mail service for the common man, and it was continued by the house of Thurn und Taxis until 1867.

The headquarters of the service were in Brussels (then a domain of the Holy Roman Emperor), with routes to major cities. Some of the services were quite rapid by the standards of the time: forty-four hours from Brussels to Paris, later cut to thirty-six; Brussels to Innsbruck, five days; Brussels to Rome, ten and one-half days. The web of Thurn und Taxis covered northwest, central, and southern Europe, was linked to England, and even reached, through Spain, the Spanish possessions in America.

For four hundred years the direction of the service remained firmly in the hands of family members, who grew immensely rich. During the earlier part of the Thirty Years War (1618–48) the business was run by a woman, Countess Alexandrine Thurn und Taxis, who, while acting as regent for her minor son, directed the vast operation. It lost none of its efficiency and prestige under her governance during this period of destructive warfare in central Europe.

The steady disintegration of the Holy Roman Empire during the late

28

22. One of three known Thurn und Taxis covers bearing the red 8-ring cancellation, 1852.

23. A cover reflecting the fruitless journey of a letter sent through the Thurn und Taxis posts at Gotha, Germany, on May 15, 1858, to Milwaukee. It reached New York on June 30—the "N. York" marking. The stamped "Advertised" indicates it was listed in a Milwaukee newspaper, the practice in those days for uncalled-for mail. The lack of response caused it to be returned to Germany on September 2, 1858.

eighteenth century and its final demise in 1806 gradually limited the Thurn und Taxis services; more and more governments took the postal services of their countries into their own hands. But in the first half of the nineteenth century the routes were still extensive enough to justify the princes in producing their own stamped paper—franked envelopes in 1847 and postage stamps in 1852.

On the first day of July, 1867, the long history of the Thurn und Taxis postal service ended in its being absorbed first by the kingdom of Prussia and a few months later by the North German Postal Union (formed on January 1, 1868). The princes of Thurn und Taxis received the enormous indemnity of three million thalers for peaceably surrendering their postal routes, buildings, and equipment.

A possibly apocryphal story concerns the Thurn und Taxis family and the government of Belgium. According to this story, when the postal service ceased in 1867, Belgium granted the family franking privileges, meaning that no postage was charged on any mail they sent. A "little trouble" resulted in the cutting off of the privilege in 1906. At the time, one of the Thurn und Taxis castles was under repair, and Belgian officials learned that building materials for it were being shipped by post—franked.

24. Area served by Thurn und Taxis during the period that the service used adhesive stamps (1852–67).

25. Military letter of July 7, 1514, sent from Campo del Brentella to the Council of Ten, in Venice. Among the first special-delivery letters, indicated by the four *Citos* within the large "C." The five triangular stirrups indicate changes of horse; the three gallows warn against delaying the mail.

IN THE EARLIEST TIMES, postal services were organized primarily as royal courier posts. The Thurn und Taxis service, as we have seen, was originally devoted to the needs of rulers and officials. The growth in the population of Europe during the Renaissance meant an increase in the number of people needing to communicate with each other. Merchants in prosperous towns found it essential to correspond with tradesmen in other communities and sent out their own couriers, the "expressmen" of the day. Messenger services were also organized by some of the guilds that were so important in town life. The butchers, in particular, traveled widely, seeking livestock for slaughter, and members of their guild delivered mail from town to town on their daily or weekly travels, often heralding their arrival with a blast from a bugle, ancestor of the post horn.

The universities, organizing from the ninth century on, employed couriers, providing means for their students to communicate with their homes, which were frequently at great distances, and with other universities. Travel was neither easy nor safe in those days, and there were no long vacations: students usually remained with their studies until they were completed. Messenger services were a profitable business through the fees paid by correspondents.

Monasteries also developed their own posts. Messengers traveling

People's Posts Begin Early

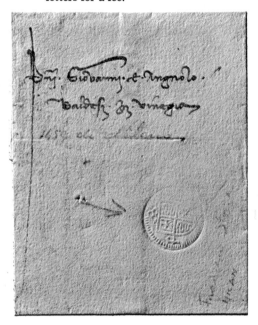

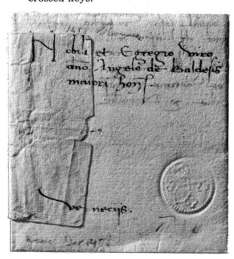

from one religious community to another were entrusted with communications written on parchment bearing news and instructions. The sheets of the parchment were wrapped around a roll, forming a scroll that passed from monastery to monastery. When it arrived at another monastery, the scroll was read aloud to the assembled monks. Replies and new messages, also written on parchment, were sewn onto the lengthening scroll and sent along to yet other monasteries, each adding messages.

An early advance in postal service was developed in the fourteenth century by Gian Galeazzo Visconti, duke of Milan from 1378 to 1402. By his orders a *staffetta* (horse post) was organized. Rome, too, developed a service to handle the papal correspondence. Some of these letters from the Italian states bore embossed marks of the rulers—stamped dry, since there were no ink pads. These are considered by some historians to be the earliest postmarks, though that distinction is given by most historians to the round hand stamp invented in 1661 by Postmaster General Henry Bishop of Great Britain (see page 17).

Another duke of Milan, Filippo Maria Visconti, who was the son of Gian Galeazzo and ruled from the death of his father until 1447, was also interested in bettering the post. From this era dates the beginning of "special delivery" pen marks to indicate the need for urgency in handling. An example is:

Postantur diu noctuque non celeriter sed fulminantissimo per cavalarum sub pena mille furcarus. Cito, Cito, Cito, Cito, Cito, Cito. Datum Mediolani hors XXII.

(To be carried day and night, not swiftly but with flying speed by the postal courier under pain of a thousand lashes. Haste, Haste, Haste, Haste, Haste, Haste. Given at Milan at twenty-two o'clock.)

The Sforza family, who succeeded the Visconti as dukes of Milan, reorganized the *staffetta*. Their new post, which began under Francesco Sforza about 1458, used a stamp that embossed the legend *Cursores Mediolanum* (Milan Couriers). This service may have been connected with that managed by the house of Thurn und Taxis.

The letters sent by merchant, monastic, university, or royal post were sheets of paper folded and sealed on the back with a wax wafer and impressed with colorless embossings made by signet rings or seals. The envelope was not invented until the first third of the nineteenth century.

Prepaid letter sheets were instituted in Paris in 1653 by Jean-Jacques Renouard de Villayer under privilege granted by Louis XIV. This service provided *billets de port payé* (prepaid postage tickets), which were wrappers for enclosing letters which were then deposited in mailboxes set up around the city. These mailboxes were cleared three times a day, the letters delivered to the central post office, the *billets* removed (so they could not be used again), and the letters sent on their way. The *billets* must have been carefully destroyed, for no examples of the Villayer wrappers are known to exist today.

The seventeenth-century poet Jean Loret described the Paris *petite poste* ("little" because it handled only city mail) in these lines translated by Richard M. Graf:

Soon there will come into existence,
For public convenience,
A certain business venture,
For the city of Paris only,
Whereby numerous boxes
Will be placed in large and little streets,
Where a person or his servant
May bring one's packages;
At any hour, there may be placed within
Notices, notes, letters of all types
Which employees
Will seek and fetch
In order to—with skill and dexterity—
Deliver them throughout the town
To nephews, cousins
Who live a distance away,
To sons-in-law, to fathers-in-law,
To sisters, to gossips,
To John, Martin, William, Luke,
To clerks, to attorneys,
To merchants—men and women,
To lovers of both sexes,
To friends, to business agents,
In short, to all types of people.
Those who have no man-servants or maid-servants,
No valets or domestics,
Will thus feel very much more at ease,
About friends who live far away.
In addition, I say and announce,
That in case a reply is required,
One can be obtained by the same method,
And, if one wishes to know how much
The postage for a letter will be,
An item which we must not omit,
In order that no one be mistaken about it,
I would like to say it will cost only one sou.

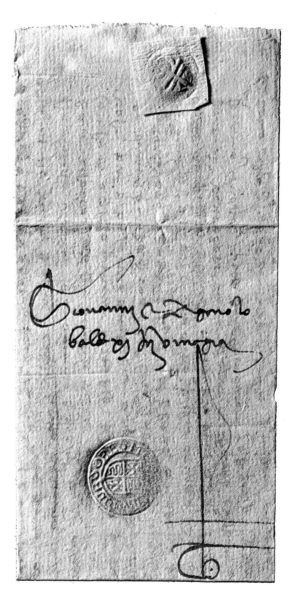

29. Embossed seal (bottom of envelope) of the *Cursores Mediolanum*, the Milan Couriers, c. 1458. Considered by some postal historians to be the world's first postmark. At the top is the letter writer's guild mark. The vertical pen stroke with crossed bars and loop indicates that postage has been paid.

30, 31. A Sardinian letter sheet of 1819 (actual size). Watermarks can be seen in the center and around the edges.

The *petite poste* was popular with Parisians, but the project failed, partly because the mailboxes became receptacles for refuse and homes for rats that ate the letters.

SARDINIA AND VENICE

The idea of prepaid letter sheets remained alive despite the failure of the Parisian system. The kingdom of Sardinia introduced them at the beginning of the nineteenth century. Sardinia was the name used for the domains of the House of Savoy, including the island and the mainland provinces of Savoy, Nice, Piedmont, Montferrat, Genoa, and part of Lombardy. The Sardinian post was a royal monopoly.

Early in 1819 Sardinia released letter sheets measuring about 10 by 15 inches for use only on the mainland. At first these were imprinted in ink with round, oval, and octagonal devices, each of which contained a horse bearing a cherub-like rider blowing a post horn. Later these devices were embossed on ornately watermarked sheets called *cavallini* (from *cavallo,* horse). The paper was watermarked with an elaborate crowned eagle in the center bearing on its breast the Cross of Savoy. Above

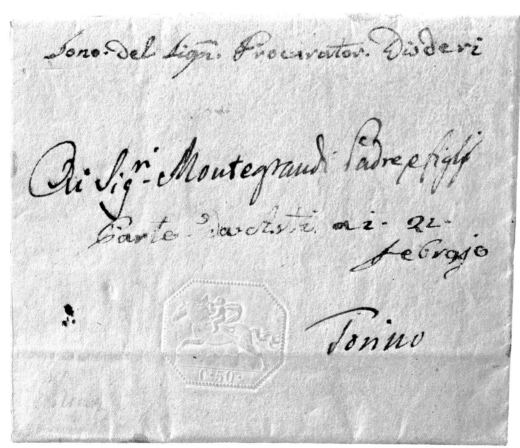

32

32. The face of the letter sheet with the embossed seal denoting its denomination.

33. An enlargement of the embossed seal on the letter sheet.

33

N 699 2

A   Q

DE Ordine dell'Illuſtriſſimi Signori Savij, & Eſſecutori alle Acque iuſta la Deliberatione per Sue Signorie Illuſtriſſime preſa ſotto li 12. Novembre 1608. per il Dacio delli Soldi 4. per Lettera, ſi commette à cadauno Cancelliero delle Cancellarie del Stato Noſtro, che per l'avvenire non dia riſpoſta, nè eſecutione à niuna ſorte di Le tere, che li ſaranno ſcritte per cadaun Officio, & Magiſtrato di queſta Città, eccetuati però li Eccellentiſſ. Conſegli, Colleggi & l'Officio Illuſtriſſ. dell'Avogaria, Auditori Novi, Noviſſimi, & Vecchi, & li Conſervatori delle Leggi, ſe non ſaranno ogn'una di eſſe Lettere incluſe, overo ſcritte in uno delli preſenti Noſtri mezi fogli ſtampati, & numerati, & ſe ſaranno incluſe più d'una ſol Lettera debbanno le ſudette Cancellarie inuiarle all'Officio Noſtro ſotto pena di Ducati 100. per cadauna volta, che contrataranno da eſſer diviſa conforme alla Delberatione ſudetta, & ancora ſieno tenuti a maggior pene, dovendo il tutto infilzar, & l'iſteſſa Deliberatione ſara anco oſſervata dallisudetti Offici, & Magiſtrati di queſta Città, ſotto le pene in eſſe dichiarite eccetuati li ſopranominati Officj.

34. A Venice "AQ" letter sheet, 1738.

and below was an inscription reading *Direzione Generale/Delle Regie Poste* (Director General's Office of the Royal Post). Around the edges, within a broken-line border and surrounding the entire sheet in outline capital letters, were the words *Corrispondenza Autorizzata In Corso Particulare Per Pedoni Ed Altre Occasioni* (Correspondence authorized to be carried privately by runner). In other words, the user had paid to send his letter, but he himself had to arrange for its carriage.

Purists argue that the Sardinia sheets were only taxes, for no postal service was provided. Even so, the Sardinian *cavallini* are important historic documents in the development of the postage stamp.

The Republic of Venice had a long postal history. A maritime state trading everywhere along the Adriatic and Mediterranean seas, it also had couriers to the inland cities of Europe and maintained connections with the Thurn und Taxis routes. Like other states, it used the mails to raise funds. From very early in the seventeenth century until almost two hundred years thereafter, anyone writing to the governmental agencies of the republic had to use a *taglio*, a special sheet of paper which cost four *soldi*, that is, a penny or two. Intergovernmental correspondence also had to be written on a *taglio*.

These Venetian letter sheets are known as the "AQ" sheets, for printed across the top on the left side of the winged lion of St. Mark, symbol of the city, was the letter *A*, while on the right was the letter *Q*. These initials referred to the Water Commission, *Aqua*, for obvious reasons an extremely important office in Venice. Beneath was a legend explaining how to use the sheets, which measured about 8 by 11½ inches. Many printers produced them during the nearly two centuries (1609–1797) they were in use.

Some students of postal history feel that these early Venetian stationery forms, like the Sardinian letter sheets, are, strictly speaking, fiscal items rather than postal stationery.

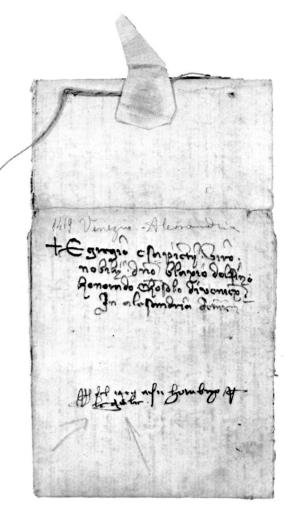

35. Letter sent from Venice to Alexandria, 1419. The cross invokes God's aid for safe carriage. The wax seal holds the end of the string tied around the letter.

36
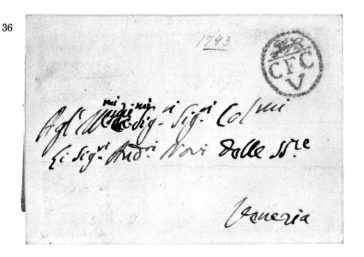

37

36, 37. Private courier letters from Verona, c. 1790. "CFC" stands for Compagnia fra Corrieri; "V" for Venice.

20 April 1823.

Välborne
Herr Lieutenanten
C. G. Treffenberg
Göteborg

38. A reconstruction by P. G. Heurgren of Curry Gabriel Treffenberg's suggested Swedish postage stamps of 1823 and their "cancel" (the address written into the inked stamp).

A SWEDISH WRAPPER

In the seventeenth century an uncomplicated postal service was organized in Sweden. On February 20, 1636, the regency governing the country for the ten-year-old Queen Christina published an "Ordinance of Post-Messengers" by which a letter was to be transmitted anywhere within the country for a fee of two *öre*, which the postmaster was to "enjoy and retain for industriousness in his appointment." No bookkeeping, no accounting!

That simple system did not last. Only a few years later, there came into force a complicated postal rate structure based on the weight of a letter, the distance it had to travel, and the number of post offices handling it. Postmasters were to be salaried. Much bookkeeping, much accounting!

After nearly three centuries a suggestion was made by a former army lieutenant, Curry Gabriel Treffenberg, for the reform of this cumbersome system. In 1823 Treffenberg, who preceded the British postal reformer Rowland Hill by fourteen years, urged, as Hill later did, the issue of a wrapper "the size of a sheet of writing paper . . . strong but not coarse, and in it a ring-shaped design readily discernible for hampering counterfeiting; also some light-colored nuance should be applied to it."

Treffenberg further recommended that "in the center of the sheet there should be two stamps side by side, occupying together an area of six square inches; one stamp deeply pressed [embossed] into the paper, and the other printed with ink. Both are to contain, besides some appropriate emblem difficult to imitate, the value of the sheet. An assortment of denominations should be according to requirements."

The letter sheet was to be folded so that the stamps showed on the outside, and the address so written that a portion of it would cover the stamps, acting as a cancellation to prevent reuse of the wrapper. Treffenberg would have eliminated the postmark, recommending that "a notation alongside the date when the letter was mailed would perhaps also be necessary: whereas there is considered to be no necessity, as heretofore customary, for marking the name of the place from which it is dispatched."

Treffenberg's carefully thought-out plan was rejected by the Swedish government. Because Sweden's postal rate structure was so complicated, too many varied-denomination sheets would have been required. A similar opinion was held in England when Rowland Hill first suggested reforming the postal system.

Despite these failures, the times were ready in the first third of the nineteenth century for postal reform. Postage was too expensive. Many correspondents managed to find cheaper ways to send their letters and avoided paying any postage. The European nations were growing in population, and their economies were expanding rapidly; postal systems were antiquated and were not keeping pace with industrial development. Soon Great Britain, Switzerland, and other countries would begin to issue adhesive stamps. Sweden's first issue appeared in 1855.

39, 40. *above*: Envelope bearing the impression of the round hand stamp invented in 1661 by Henry Bishop, Master of the Posts to Charles II of England. The stamp, which notes month and date of mailing, is generally recognized as the first postmark. *below*: An American Bishop Mark, believed unique, from Savannah, c. 1765.

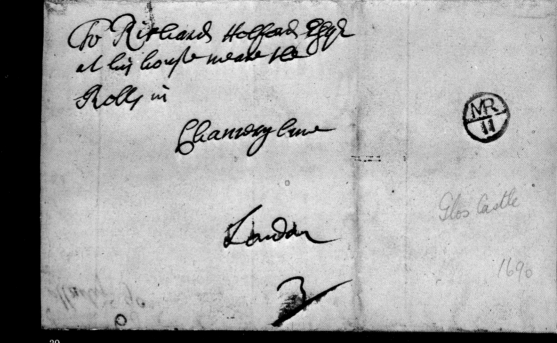

39

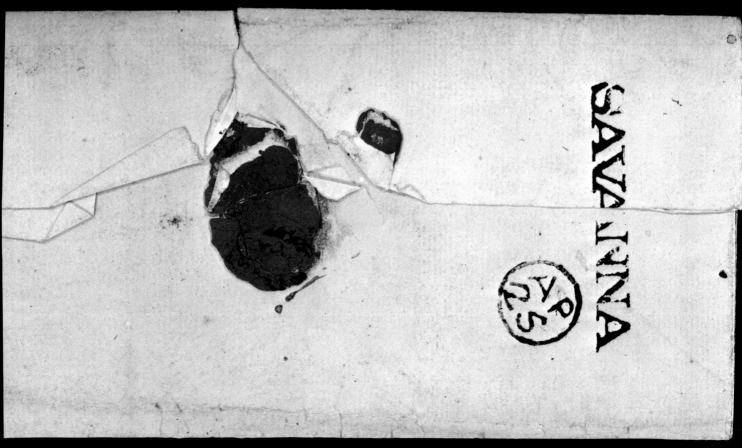

40

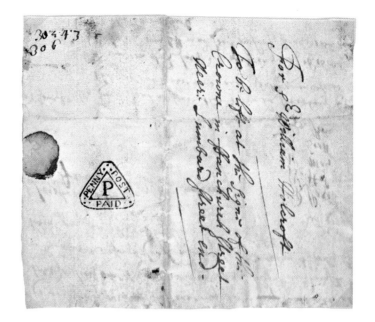

41. Private entrepreneurs William Dockwra and Robert Murray established a local delivery service in London in 1680, with a distinctive postal marking indicating date and time.

The Stamp Comes to England

THE POSTAL SERVICE of the princes of Thurn und Taxis, although extensive and important, was by no means the only post operating in Europe. From late medieval times many national governments maintained their own mail service, France having the largest. England also had its own; it was in England that many of the important advances were made in bettering postal service, and England introduced the postage stamp.

Royal courier service was long established in England, but these couriers were sent only by the express order of the king as occasion demanded and not on a regular basis.

England's first Governor of the King's Post, appointed by Henry VIII in 1516, was Brian Tuke. He served for nearly thirty years until his death in 1545, working to improve the service, which was still only a royal horse post. Tuke's innovation was to set up post relay stations with fresh horses at intervals of about twenty miles; his inspiration was drawn from the ancient Persian relay system of post-riders. The towns were responsible for providing the horses; needless to say, as the post did not benefit them, they were reluctant to do so.

By the time of Elizabeth I, a few letters other than the government's were being carried by the post. It also carried people, that is, the facilities of horses and relay were used by all those traveling on the queen's business. Naturally, it was a great temptation to any traveler to declare himself on a royal errand. There were also private carrier lines that transported passengers, freight, and letters.

In 1637, in the reign of Charles I, Thomas Witherings was appointed Master of the Posts. Witherings established the first postage system in

England, working out a system of charges based on the weight of a letter and the distance it was sent. Mail traveled by carrier wagons, coaches, horse, and foot post.

Charles II's Master of the Posts was Henry Bishop. Bishop's name is famous in the history of stamps because he invented the postmark as it is known today. It was described thus: "A stamp is invented that is putt upon every letter shewing the day of the moneth that every letter comes to the office, so that no letter carryer may dare to detayne a letter from post to post; which before was usual." The Bishop Mark, first used in 1661, was a circular hand stamp that included the month and the date of mailing; it remained in use in England, Scotland, Ireland, the American colonies, and India until 1787.

All the postal services mentioned above were geared to the delivery of letters to a distant place. Within the towns and cities, even London, there was room for improvement. Strangely enough, to send a letter within the city it was necessary either to dispatch one's servant with it or hire a messenger. Labor was then very inexpensive and without doubt most people able to write a letter had a servant to take it or could afford a messenger. The difficulty lay in the fact that houses were not numbered, and it was difficult for a messenger to find a given household unless he was very familiar with the neighborhood.

In the late seventeenth century William Dockwra, a London merchant, and Robert Murray, an upholsterer, decided to establish a local post in London as a private, commercial enterprise. They set up the amazing number of 450 receiving offices for mail, with 7 sorting offices and deliveries to the recipients' door. They chose to open their service on what one would have thought a rather inauspicious day—April 1, 1680.

Letters and parcels were carried by the Dockwra service from one part of London to another for a penny. Since the mail was supposed to be delivered within one hour of its receipt at the office, they were postmarked with the exact time as well as the date. Letters could be insured for up to ten pounds. Dockwra soon employed more people than the General Post Office run by the government, which even in 1690 had only 316 employees in all of Great Britain.

Such was the origin of the celebrated "Penny Post," but it had only a short life under Dockwra. Revenues from the government posts were assigned to members of the royal family or royal favorites as perquisites. The Penny Post naturally whittled down these revenues. Dockwra's services were therefore absorbed by the government in 1682.

Under the government the London Penny Post functioned for many years after Dockwra's death in 1716; it became the Two Penny Post in 1801, reverting to the Penny Post when the first stamps were issued in

1840. After 175 years this mail service was discontinued in 1855, being incorporated into the General Post Office as the London District Post.

Penny posts were born in other British communities. Services began to cross the country between towns and linked with the major city mails. Letters began to be carried not by single horsemen but by mail coaches, the first coach running in 1784 between Bristol (then one of the largest cities in England) and London.

Although mail service was slowly improving, postage, except for the penny posts within the cities, was extremely expensive. The cost of the letter was still based on the number of miles it had to travel and on the number of sheets within its wrappers—candled at post offices much as the old-time grocer candled an egg. Much craft was exercised by the British in avoiding payment of postage. Some forged the franks of members of Parliament, who had the privilege of sending mail postage-free. Since the recipient paid the postage on receipt, codes between correspondents were devised—the style of an address might indicate "all is well" or "come at once," and the postman often had to take letters back to the post office when they were refused by a recipient who had got a message from the appearance of the letter alone. It was not unusual for a person with several friends in a single community to write each of them a letter on a single large sheet of paper; the recipient cut the letters apart and handed them to the other correspondents. Letters having a London destination were sent secretly in batches to the city by wagon and then put into the much cheaper Penny Post. The mails had become extremely profitable for the government, and all this ingenuity in escaping payment was exceedingly irritating to the post-office bureaucracy.

The postage rates were absurdly high. It cost 13 pence to send a "single letter," meaning one with only one sheet, three to four hundred miles, and added to this heavy basic charge were many surcharges. Heavier letters cost two or three times as much.

THE SCHOOLMASTER FROM KIDDERMINSTER

The British Post Office was reformed by Sir Rowland Hill, and his reforms led directly to the issuance of the world's first postage stamp. Hill's is the most important single name in the history of stamps.

Rowland Hill (1795–1879) was born at Kidderminster near Birmingham. He came from a family of energetic educators and reformers: his parents founded a progressive school called Hazelwood in which their five sons and two daughters taught, beginning while they were still teenagers. Hill himself was an educator for many years and was middle-aged when he began to be interested in postal reform and to take steps to re-

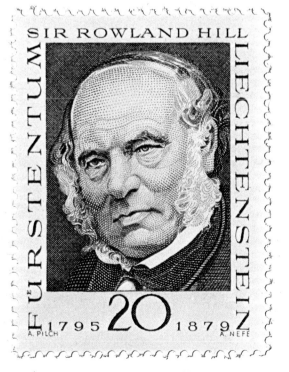

42. Sir Rowland Hill, honored as a pioneer of philately on a 1968 issue of Liechtenstein.

43

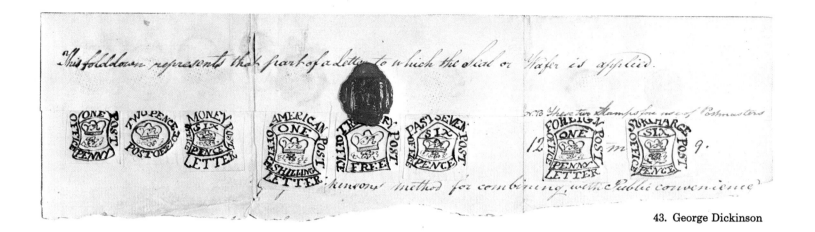

43. George Dickinson

43–47. Some of the 2,600
designs entered in the British
Treasury Competition for the
first adhesive postage stamp.
Dickinson proposed, among
other things, stamps
designating destination.
Whiting contributed more
than a hundred suggestions,
all colorful. A number of the
designs included embossed
stamps.

form the postal system. He had many additional interests in his life: the rotary press, astronomy, architecture, navigation.

In 1837 Hill published a pamphlet entitled *Post Office Reform: Its Importance and Practicability* in which he advocated the prepayment of postage by means either of envelopes imprinted with a stamp or, alternatively, labeled with "bits of paper just large enough to bear the stamp and covered at the back with a glutinous wash." He also urged a uniform rate of charges for letters, with no charge for extra sheets. The Post Office bureaucracy was, not surprisingly, hostile to the reformer's proposals, but Hill had powerful allies, especially among the merchants and the press. To the opponents of reform, headed by the postmaster general, who said that the low charges would bankrupt the Post Office by reducing revenue, Hill replied that cheaper postage would increase the government's income. He pointed out that when taxes had been lowered on coffee and tea, the consumption of these commodities had increased so markedly that the government had actually obtained more revenue.

Prepaid letter sheets were not in fact a new idea. As mentioned earlier, they were used in France as early as 1653 and in Sardinia in 1818. Their use in those countries, however, had been in the nature of an experiment that did not last.

The adhesive postage itself was not at first central to Hill's arguments. His pamphlet proposed something akin to today's air-letter sheet. His device for prepayment of postage was that "stamped . . . covers and sheets of paper be supplied to the public . . . and sold at such a price as to include the postage . . . [and that] letters so stamped [be] treated in all respects as franks." He wrote also that "covers at various prices would be required for packets of various weights."

44. Charles Whiting

45. Charles Whiting

46. Robert W. Sievier

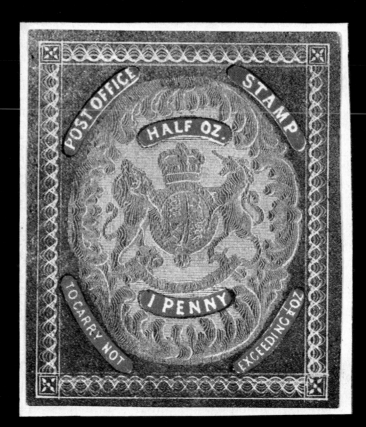

47. Myers & Company

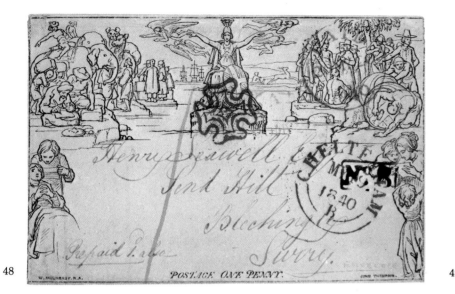

48, 49. Two William Mulready envelopes showing various cancellations. The cover at left bears a Maltese cross and the one at right, a manuscript "2."

50, 51. Two of the many caricatures by various illustrators indicating the ridicule heaped on the Mulready envelope.

By 1839, the short space of two years after Hill's pamphlet, the Post Office had given up the struggle against reform, and Hill was told to proceed with his plans. Hill commissioned William Mulready, a well-known painter and member of the Royal Academy, to make a design for wrappers and envelopes. It was not a happy choice. Mulready produced a fussy design, overloaded with symbols, that aroused much hilarity and had to be withdrawn. Hill also held a public competition in which artists were invited to proffer designs for stamps. There were no fewer than 2,600 entries, and four prizes were awarded, but the design finally chosen

52. The Penny Black, the word's first adhesive postage stamp, designed by Henry Corbould after a medal of Queen Victoria by William Wyon. Issued by Great Britain in 1840.

was that of Henry Corbould, who was not a contestant. Corbould's design was adapted from William Wyon's medal of the young Queen Victoria. The stamps, a Penny Black and a Two Pence Blue, were engraved by Charles Heath and his son Frederick and were produced by a process for printing steel engravings invented by the American Jacob Perkins, who worked in London as a bank-note printer. The background selected for the stamps was an intricately patterned lathework. These portraits-in-miniature remain to this day classics of the engraver's art and gems of philatelic art.

53. During a visit to England in the 1850s to press his campaign for peace and universal brotherhood, Elihu Burritt, the "learned blacksmith" of New Britain, Connecticut, instituted a plan for cheap world-wide postage called the "Ocean Penny Postage." This illustrated envelope, in the style of the Mulready envelopes, was one of many issued.

54   55

54, 55. Peruvian stamps depicting a *quipu*, the knotted message string, and an Indian message bearer. The *quipu* commemorates an international stamp exhibition, Exfilbra, held in 1972, and the runner marks the Munich Olympics of the same year.

THE INDIANS OF AMERICA failed to develop a written language. Such communication as existed was by primitive devices such as smoke signals and sign language. Pictographs—stylized pictures on rocks, tree bark, hides, or in modern times, paper—also conveyed simple ideas. Letters containing pictographic writing were used by the North American Indians as late as the nineteenth century, and pictographs were also used by the Aztecs of Mexico: when Cortez's conquistadors landed in Vera Cruz in 1519, Aztec couriers brought pictographs describing them to their ruler, Montezuma, in Tenochititlán (present-day Mexico City). Glyphs, pictorial or conventionalized symbols, some of which may have represented syllables, were used by the Maya and a few other groups in Mexico.

Both the Aztecs and the Incas in Peru used couriers to carry their messages. The Aztecs had relay stations which were located about ten miles apart, and teams could deliver messages with amazing speed.

The Inca couriers also ran in relay. Because so much of the Inca domain was mountainous, steps were chiseled along the roads to facilitate passage through the mountains. The Inca runners carried an extraordinary device for conveying simple messages, the *quipu*, a string cord from which hung strands of different colors tied in knots. Each color had a specific meaning, as gold, silver, horses, or wheat, and the knots represented definite numbers.

Only seventeen years after the landing of the Pilgrims, the English colonies established a postal system on the North American continent.

The
New World

49

56, 57. Recalling in 1970 the 350th anniversary of the Pilgrims' voyage to North America, Britain commemorated their departure. Later that year the United States took note of the Pilgrims' arrival off Plymouth.

In 1639 the Massachusetts General Court appointed one Richard Fairbanks as postmaster for the colony:

> For preventing the miscarriage of letters . . . it is ordered that notice be given that Richard Fairbanks at his house in Boston is the place appointed for all letters, which are brought from beyond the seas or are to be sent hither, are to be brought to him, and he is to take care that they be delivered, or sent according to his directions; and he is allowed for every such letter one pence and must answer all miscarriages through his own neglect in this kind; provided that no man shall be compelled to bring his letters thither except he please.

Fairbanks's postal facility was a convenience—a drop for depositing letters for transmission overseas and for picking up letters that had arrived by ship or a message left by a traveler. There were no letter carriers, but mail that remained uncalled-for at the postmaster's could be delivered for a charge.

In 1685 Edward Randolph was appointed the first postmaster for the English colonies. In 1691 William III named Thomas Neale to establish a new colonial postal system. Neale never set foot in the colonies, but employed as his deputy in America Andrew Hamilton, governor of New Jersey, who made his headquarters in Philadelphia. Although Hamilton instituted a service that ran from New Hampshire to Virginia, he could not interest the colonies in amalgamating their postal facilities. Most colonial entrepreneurs preferred their own rate structure and income to uniting their services under the New Jersey governor.

Water-borne communications remained by far the most satisfactory, the various colonies being connected by sailing ship service carrying mail and passengers. In 1710 Queen Anne established New York as general headquarters for the royal post in America, but some years were to pass before it became active. A 1729 map by H. Moll contained this legend of the service:

> An account of ye post of ye continent of Nth America as they were regulated by ye Postmasters Genl of ye Post House. The Western Post setts out from Philadelphia every Friday leaving Letters at Burlington and Perth Amboy and arrives at New York on Sunday night; the distance between Philadelphia and New York being 106 miles. The Post goes out Eastward every Monday morning from New York, and arrives at Seabrook [Saybrook, Conn.] Thursday noon; being 150 miles where the Post from Boston setts out at the same time; the New York Post returning with the Eastern letters, and the Boston Post with the Western. Bags are dropt at New London, Stommington [Stonington, Conn.], Rhode

58. A letter from Robert Livingston, founder of the distinguished American family from Albany, New York, to his brother Andrew Russell in Rotterdam, September 26, 1677. Endorsement at lower left, "p. Catalyntis R. Elslant," is that of the man who carried the letter to Mr. Russell.

59. The back of a folded cover that was sent c. 1765 from Williamsburg, Virginia, to Gov. Samuel Ward of Rhode Island. It is franked on the face by "Botetourt" (Norborne Berkeley, Baron de Botetourt, later governor of Virginia).

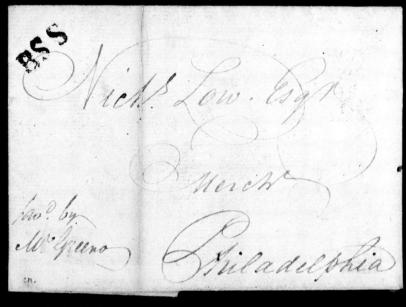

60. A Revolutionary War cover sent from Newburyport, Massachusetts, to Philadelphia, January 23, 1776.

61. Probably the earliest private-express cover in America, headed "Balto., October 18th, 1783." "B.S.S." stands for Baltimore Stage Service.

62

63

62, 63. The first United States postage stamps, the 5c Franklin and the 10c Washington, issued in 1847, both designed by James Parsons Major. The 5c was adapted from an engraving by Richard W. Dodson, and the 10c from an engraving by Asher Brown Durand. Both engravings appeared in Joseph Delaplaine's *Repository of the Lives and Portraits of Distinguished American Characters* (Philadelphia, 1815).

64, 65. Two blocks, both the largest multiples known, of the first United States postage stamps, each valued in 1974 at between $125,000 and $150,000.

64

65

66

66, 67. While modern covers canceled on the first day of issue are plentiful, postal historians are constantly on the alert for first-day or near-first-day cancellations of nineteenth-century stamps.

The first United States postage stamps had their initial sale in New York on July 1, 1847, and until recently the two envelopes at left—the 5c Franklin with cancellation of July 1, 1847, and the 10c Washington, canceled July 9, 1847, were the earliest known uses of the two stamps.

In the early 1970s, however, Harry Mark, an Indianapolis tax consultant, purchased a law library. In January 1972, using a volume of Burns' *Annotated Indiana Statutes*, he found in it the cover below, bearing a date of July 2, 1847. The envelope still contained the original material; its weight indicated why there was a manuscript "10" in the upper right corner—the two 10c stamps were insufficient postage. Although the two stamps had been given a red-grid cancellation, the post-office clerk, after inscribing the "10" for postage due, also added pen marks to the stamps.

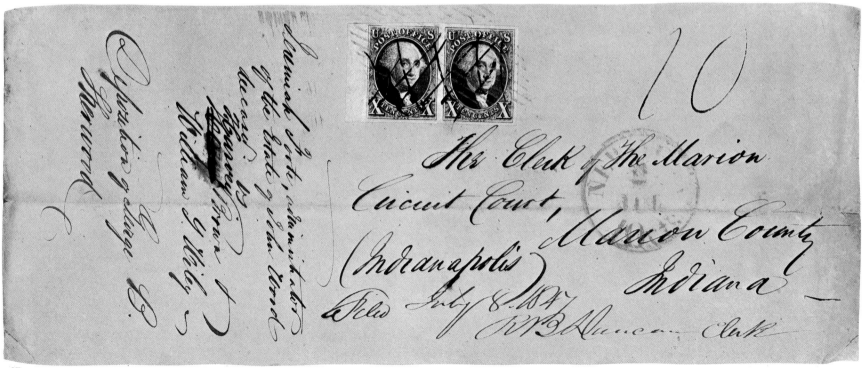

67

Island, and Bristol. The Post from Boston to Piscataway (near Portsmouth) being 70 miles leaves Letters at Ipswich, Salem, Marblehead and Newberry. There are offices keept at Burlington, Perth Amboy in New Jersey, New London and Stommington in Connecticut, at Rhode Island, Bristol, Ipswich, Salem, Marblehead and Newberry, and the 3 Great offices are at Boston, New York & Philadelphia.

After Andrew Hamilton, several men held the postmaster position until in 1753 Benjamin Franklin, who had already established himself as a publisher, was appointed to the office, sharing it with William Hunter of Williamsburg, Virginia. Franklin was very busy, visiting post offices in the North and South, raising productivity, and turning a profit, one of the few ever recorded in American postal operations. He held the post until 1774, when he was removed for siding with his fellow Americans who were protesting against the policies of the king and Parliament.

THE STAMP ACT AND ITS CONSEQUENCES

A stamp changed the course of history; not a postage stamp, but a tax stamp that aroused the ire of the American colonists. There was a long history of colonial opposition to what were regarded as unfair parliamentary acts by which the British government required the colonists to pay various taxes which were used primarily for military defense. The Stamp Act of 1765 was the most irritating of these. It meant that a revenue stamp had to be bought and affixed to legal and commercial papers, pamphlets, newspapers, almanacs, playing cards, and dice. The Stamp Act revenues were to provide funds for, among other things, the maintenance of British troops in America.

The stamps themselves bore the legend "America" surmounting a crown resting on a crossed sword and scepter within a circular garter inscribed *Honi soit qui mal y pense* (Evil be to him who evil thinks), the motto of the Order of the Garter, and the denomination. Some were to be embossed on documents; others, of similar design but smaller, were to be printed on the paper used for newspapers and pamphlets.

The editor of the Boston *Evening Post* referred to the tax stamp on the corner of documents as "the pretty bird" and remarked, "Although this emblem has but little in't, you must e'en take it or you'l have no print." Most colonists, however, refused to take the humorous view.

A Stamp Act Congress was held in New York City in October 1765, to petition George III and Parliament to rescind the tax. The act was rescinded on February 22, 1766, but by 1767 Parliament had devised new stamp duties—on glass, paper, paints, lead, and tea—that were equally

72. The Benjamin Franklin 1c, 1851. Designed by Edward Purcell after the bust by Jean-Antoine Houdon. The pair shown are among the rarest examples known of the issue because the scrollwork around the portrait is complete. Most examples show this ornamentation trimmed off.

74

73, 74. The Thomas Jefferson 5c, 1851. Designed by Edward Purcell after an engraving by John B. Forrest. The pair on the cover are extraordinary because of their wide margins.

75. One of two known unused blocks of four of the Thomas Jefferson 5c, 1851. Valued in 1974 at more than $18,000.

76

77

78

79

80

76. A unique color variety—the 5c "buff" Jefferson of 1861, valued in 1976 at more than $16,000. The value is so high because only the first printing was in buff; later printings resulted in various shades of brown. The stamp was designed by James McDonnough after an engraving by John B. Forrest.

77. One of the largest known unused blocks of the 12c Washington of 1851, an Edward Purcell design adapted from an Asher B. Durand engraving after a painting by Gilbert Stuart.

78–80. Rare unperforated pairs of stamps from an 1857–61 series, all Edward Purcell designs, the 24c Washington from a portrait by Gilbert Stuart, the 30c Franklin from the bust by Jean-Antoine Houdon, and the 90c Washington from an Asher B. Durand engraving based on a painting by John Trumbull.

81. Cover showing the 1851 Washington bisected. When there was a shortage of stamps of small denominations, those of larger value, such as this 12c, were often cut in two diagonally, horizontally, or vertically.

81

disturbing. The colonists responded by placing an embargo on these items, and eventually the British withdrew the duties on them, with the exception of the one on tea, on which the embargo remained. The tea duty was a continuing source of irritation, culminating on December 16, 1773, in the famous Boston Tea Party, in which colonists dressed as Indians boarded British ships in Boston harbor and destroyed their cargo of tea. Strong British reprisals followed. These and other events brought on the Revolution. During the course of it, in 1775, Benjamin Franklin was named postmaster general of the colonies. He established service from

New England to the South, even though some British posts continued to function throughout the War for Independence.

The war ended in 1781, and in 1789 a full-fledged federal system was established, creating the United States. Congress selected Samuel Osgood of Massachusetts as the first postmaster general of the U.S. He served from 1789 to 1791.

Osgood had approximately seventy-six post offices to manage. Fifty-one of these were along the main post road, which ran along the Atlantic Coast from Maine to Georgia. In the entire country there were only 2,400 miles of post roads. The roads expanded as the country moved westward, and the number of post offices grew to the present figure of 33,000.

In the first half of the nineteenth century, local posts functioned within American cities as they did in Europe. In February 1842, Henry T. Windsor and Alexander M. Greig established the City Despatch Post in New York and, just two years after the issue of Britain's Penny Black,

82. The bicentennial of the Boston Tea Party, December 16, 1773, was observed postally somewhat early, on July 4, 1973, with the issuance of this block of four stamps designed by William A. Smith.

83, 84. The 5c Washington provisional issued by Postmaster Robert H. Morris of New York City, 1845. The envelope shows the largest known multiple, a block of nine plus an additional strip of three.

83

84

85. Postmaster James M. Buchanan's Baltimore provisional of 1845 was handstamped on covers.

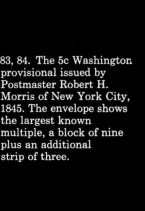

85

86. St. Louis "Bears," 20c provisional with Missouri coat of arms, 1845. Issued by Postmaster John M. Wimer.

86

87. Brattleboro provisional (5c), 1846, with initials of Postmaster Frederick N. Palmer.

87

88. Cover with the only known pair of Brattleboro provisionals.

88

89. Asa H. Waters, postmaster in Millbury, Massachusetts, used a portrait of George Washington on his 5c provisional of 1846.

89

90. Engraved 5c provisional issued in 1846 by Postmaster Welcome B. Sayles of Providence, Rhode Island.

90

ALEXANDRIA PAID 5 POST OFFICE

5

PAID

PAID

POST OFFICE FIVE CENTS

Paid

Charles J Folger Esq

Geneva

Due

PAID James M. Buchanan 10 Cents.

Nathan Smith Lincoln

Member of College

May 5 1847. Hanover

New Hampshire

POST OFFICE NEW HAVEN 5 PAID A Mitchell P.M.

Francis Markoe Jr Esqr

Washington City

POST OFFICE PAID 5

V

Hon. J. M. Barton

NAPOL APR

issued adhesive postage stamps bearing a portrait of George Washington. These were the first postage stamps in the U.S. Later in 1842 the federal government acquired the service, called it the U.S. City Despatch Post, and issued stamps with that title. These are the first U.S. governmental postage stamps, but the service was limited to New York City mails.

By 1845 the federal postmasters of New York (Robert H. Morris), Baltimore (James M. Buchanan), St. Louis (James M. Wimer), and New Haven (Edward A. Mitchell) had issued "provisional" stamps, also used for local delivery, creating pieces of mail that are today among the rarest of American letters. By 1846 postmasters in Alexandria, Va.; Annapolis, Md.; Boscowen, N.H.; Lockport, N.Y.; Millbury, Mass.; and Providence, R.I. were also issuing provisionals. In 1847 the federal government issued the first U.S. stamps intended for use throughout the country.

92. A rare pony express cover, franked by Senator Milton S. Latham of California and addressed to the secretary of the governor of the state.

THE PONY EXPRESS

As new settlers crossed the continent, the mails followed. There was ship mail around Cape Horn, mail sent over the rail route across Panama, stage-coach service, and express lines which handled an important amount of mail across the overland route. Among the successful pioneer express companies was Russell, Majors, and Waddell. Their Central Overland, California, and Pikes Peak Express Co. was organized to haul freight as earlier companies owned by the three men had. They set up a "horse express" to speed mail from a last eastern outpost, St. Joseph, Missouri, to the West and San Francisco. This was the "pony express," a short-lived gamble, a colorful moment in the history of the American West, and a business failure for its entrepreneurs.

The pony express lasted only eighteen months and was not a success, but it caught the public imagination and became famous. Its route from St. Joseph was mainly over the well-known Oregon-California trail by way of Fort Kearny, Scotts Bluff, Fort Laramie, South Pass, Fort Bridger, and Salt Lake, Carson City, and Sacramento.

In the spring of 1860, San Francisco newspapers carried this advertisement in the usual classified-ad style of the day:

93. Harold von Schmidt's 1960 stamp commemorating the centennial of the pony express.

> WANTED
>
> Young skinny wiry fellows not over eighteen.
> Must be expert riders willing to risk death daily.
> Orphans preferred. Wages $25 per week.
> Apply, Central Overland Express,
> Alta Bldg., Montgomery St.

When the young men had signed on for their lonely and dangerous missions, they also signed an agreement "not to use profane language, not to get drunk, not to gamble, not to treat animals cruelly, and not to do anything else that is incompatible with the conduct of a gentleman." There were probably more than a hundred riders, including the fifteen-year-old William F. Cody.

On April 3, 1860, the initial run was made, riders with west-bound mail taking off from St. Joseph and those with east-bound mail departing from Sacramento.

Mail on the pony express was always heavier from west to east than from east to west, and despite the high cost of $5.00 for a letter carried, the service was never financially successful. When transcontinental telegraph lines were completed on October 24, 1861, the pony express ended, although a few deliveries from St. Joseph were made as late as November 20 of that year.

The Postal Card

POSTAL CARDS WERE FIRST ISSUED in the Austro-Hungarian empire. They were the invention of Dr. Emmanuel Herrmann, who taught political economy at the Vienna-Neustadt Military Academy. He proposed that the government should introduce cards the size of envelopes with writing space to contain not more than twenty words of handwriting or print to be sent open through the post. Herrmann's proposal was accepted almost instantly by the government, and the first cards were issued in September 1869. They bore the notation "The Postal Authorities do not assume any responsibility for the contents of the written communication," a precaution against libel claims. The official wording on the cards appeared in German in combination with other languages of the empire —Hungarian, Czech, Italian, Polish, Slovenian, Ruthenian, and Illyrian —for use in the various regions.

The idea caught on quickly. Great Britain issued its first card on October 1, 1870, although a guide to manners was of the opinion that "it is questionable whether a note on a postal card is entitled to the courtesy of a response." The United States issued its first card in 1873. The American card had an imprinted head of Liberty in brown on a buff light cardboard. Since then, U.S. cards have appeared in various sizes, including at one time a "ladies' card," a smaller version of the standard issue.

"Postal card" identifies the government-issue stamp-imprinted cards. In most countries the purchaser pays only the cost of the imprinted stamp for the card. "Postcard" is the term that refers to commercially produced cards such as picture postcards, to which an adhesive stamp has to be affixed.

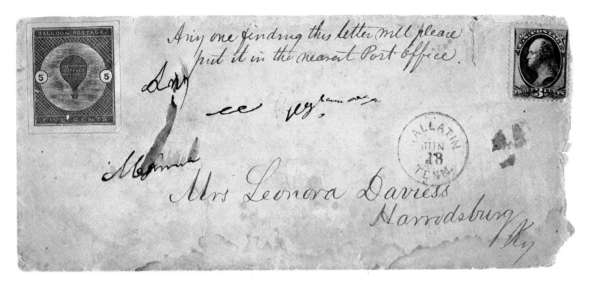

94. A classic American air-post cover, now rare, with "Buffalo" balloon unofficial label designed by Samuel Archer King, 1877. The mail was probably dropped over the side of the balloon, and the written request on this cover, "Anyone finding this letter will please put it in the nearest post office," was evidently followed by someone in Gallatin, Tennessee, judging from the postmark.

95. A cover flown out of Paris via balloon during the Franco-Prussian War.

MESSAGE-BEARING THROUGH THE AIR has ancient origins. Pigeons were said to have been employed by Alexander the Great to send word to his troops. The Chinese are reported to have utilized trained geese as well as the kite, which was also used centuries later by the British to drop propaganda leaflets on Napoleon's troops. Pigeons have been used on the Great Barrier Reef off Australia to carry messages.

The balloon was invented in 1783 by the French brothers Joseph-Michel and Jacques-Etienne Montgolfier. For nearly a century it was used to carry mail. As early as 1784 Dr. John Jeffries of Boston dropped messages from a balloon over London; and in 1793 Jean-Pierre Blanchard, a Frenchman who had flown with Dr. Jeffries, made an ascent at Philadelphia bearing a message from President Washington.

An Englishman, William Samuel Hensen, proposed in 1843 that mail be sent by air in an aerial steam carriage that unfortunately turned out to be unworkable. An American balloonist, John Wise, carried mail in 1859 on an experimental flight from St. Louis, but the packets had to be dumped over Lake Erie to gain altitude. Later the same year Wise carried some mail on a short flight from Lafayette to Crawfordsville, Indiana. His balloon, the *Jupiter,* forms the design for a U.S. stamp issued in 1959, the Post Office commemorating the centenary of this flight as the first U.S. airmail.

In 1870–71, during the Franco-Prussian War, more than fifty balloons carried mail out of besieged Paris. It was in Paris, too, that two Frenchmen used photography to reduce communications to minuscule size so they could be transported by pigeon. The same technique was used for

The Heavens Are Conquered

96

97

98

96–98. Three rare United States stamps
issued in 1930 for use on mail for the
first Europe to U.S. round-trip flight
of the *Graf Zeppelin*.

microfilming the American V-mail of World War II. The British also used the technique.

The rigid airship developed primarily by the Germans and called the dirigible was an extensive mail carrier, beginning with flights before World War I. Later, dirigibles flew around the world and made many point-to-point long-distance flights, some to the U.S. Britain and Italy also had dirigible mail, and the American-built dirigibles *Shenandoah* and *Los Angeles* carried mail in the 1920s.

The Wright brothers broke through the barrier to air travel with a heavier-than-air machine that made a brief flight over Kill Devil Hills in North Carolina in 1903, and it was not long after that the flying machine followed the runner, the horse, the stagecoach, the train, boat, balloon, and automobile as a mail carrier. By 1911, less than a decade after the Wright flight, airmail service was making its tenuous start.

On September 17, 1911, an aviator named Calbraith Perry Rodgers took off from Sheepshead Bay on Long Island, New York, for Long Beach, California. His cross-country journey of 4,311 miles took forty-nine days, but only three days, ten hours, and fourteen minutes of flying time. The zigzag flight mostly followed railroad tracks, and a special train, painted white, carried replacement equipment. The special train also provided quarters for Rodgers and his mechanics; he stopped frequently and did not fly at night. Rodgers took a southern route to avoid the Rocky Mountains, over which he could not fly. On the journey the mechanics were busy: Rodgers crashed fifteen times, and when he arrived in Long Beach he was on crutches. Legend has it that his plane, called the *Vin Fiz Flyer* after a soft drink produced by Armour, the flight's sponsor, was rebuilt so often during the journey that only the original rudder and a strut or two remained on arrival. Cal Rodgers's plane did not bear official mail, but carried letters and cards that bore "Vin Fiz" labels. These are among the rarest of philatelic items.

On September 23, 1911, only a week after Cal Rodgers began his pioneer flight, Earle Ovington took off in a Blériot monoplane, the *Dragonfly*, from an air show in Garden City, Long Island. His destination was Mineola, which was six miles away. He carried regular mail, several hundred letters and cards that were packed into a mail sack. The sack had to rest on his lap during the flight, for there was no other place for it in his craft. Arriving over Mineola seven minutes after takeoff, Ovington dropped his sack over the side to the local postmaster, who was standing in a field below him, waving a red flag. The sack almost hit the postmaster. Later, many air shows provided mail service on short flights.

Before World War I, the U.S. Congress had already been urged to

support a program for airmail development. By 1918, possibly because of successful use of the airplane in the war, Congress did approve funds for an experimental flight between Washington, D.C., Philadelphia, and New York City by Army Air Force pilots, and the Post Office issued a special twenty-four-cent stamp, a blue biplane framed in carmine. The plane was called *Jenny* after the production number "J. N.," given to it by its manufacturer, the Glen Curtiss Co. One pane of one hundred of the stamps, purchased at a Washington, D.C., branch post office, was found with its center, the plane, printed upside down. It is the most expensive U.S. postage stamp, having a value in 1976 of almost $50,000.

The plane, No. 38262 (the number may be seen on the stamp), took off from Washington, with President Woodrow Wilson and others looking on, the morning of May 15, 1918, and unfortunately, owing to a faulty compass, flew in the wrong direction.

A milepost in cross-country transport of mail was the North Platte-Omaha-Chicago night flight made by aviator Jack Knight on February 22, 1921.

Pioneer daytime airmail flights began in many countries. Italy, early in the field, issued the first airmail stamp—for a Turin-Rome flight in 1917.

Transoceanic flights were pioneered by the U.S. Navy in May 1919 with a giant "flying-boat" plane. The craft had been engineered during World War I to bomb the U-boats off the Atlantic coast, but was never used for that purpose. The flight, Newfoundland to the Azores to Portugal to England, required twenty-two days. In June of the same year two Englishmen, Capt. John Alcock and Lieut. Arthur W. Brown, flew a Vickers plane from Newfoundland to Ireland in sixteen hours, twenty-seven minutes. Charles A. Lindbergh made his solo nonstop transatlantic flight eight years later.

Attempts to speed mail from ship to shore and vice versa began in 1910, but most of them were failures. In November 1910, Eugene Ely flew a Curtiss airplane off a special deck on the U.S.S. *Birmingham*, which was off the coast near Hampton Roads, Virginia, and landed on the near-by shore. Clarence Chamberlain, a transatlantic flyer, flew a plane from the U.S.S. *Leviathan* off Fire Island to the New Jersey shore in July 1927. Two years later, the *Leviathan* was once more used for the pickup of mail by air.

On August 11, 1938, the government of republican Spain operated a submarine post between Barcelona and Mahon on the island of Minorca, a one-time effort to raise funds. Six stamps were issued for the occasion, but the fund-raising effort was not successful.

99. The wife of Calbraith Perry Rodgers, "postmistress" of the Vin Fiz flight, mailed this card to the *Dallas News* on the Waco–San Antonio stage of the flight. The postmark indicates its arrival, October 22, 1911. The message took up the space intended for the Vin Fiz label, which had to be wrapped over the top of the card.

100. One of four or five known blocks of four of the rarest United States airmail stamp, the 1918 24c with its center inverted. The block had a value in 1976 of about $170,000.

101. Envelope with a die proof of the "First Man on the Moon" stamp, with first-day-of-issue cancellation (September 9, 1969) and, below it, the "Moon" cancellation, actually applied during the return flight to earth.

To the Moon

MAN HAS BEEN TO THE MOON. So has the postage stamp. The twentieth century has brought sophistication of postal services and great changes in postage-stamp design. Mechanical devices are now doing much of the work of processing the mail.

Railroads, which in the late nineteenth century replaced horse-drawn vehicles for mail distribution, carried specially equipped cars—miniature post offices—that were used to pick up mail at way stations, sort it, and drop off sacks of mail as warranted as the train passed through the countryside. Postal buses replaced these cars; they are still used in several countries.

In America trolley cars once operated between branch post offices in several cities and between cities. Mail was sorted as the cars wended their way through the streets. A mailbox was hooked on the rear for the passing citizen to drop in his letters. Rural free delivery was inaugurated in the U.S. just before the turn of the century and still functions today.

Late in the nineteenth century, a subterranean pneumatic-tube delivery service functioned between branch post offices in New York, Philadelphia, Chicago, London, Berlin, Rome, Vienna, Paris, and several other large cities of the world. There were extensive facilities by which mail was distributed between branches to speed delivery to recipients. Some cities maintained special posting boxes on some routes. Special postal cards, mailing wrappers, and envelopes permitted mail users to take advantage of the fast service. World War II bombings knocked out some of these services in Europe, and most have been abandoned. None functions in the United States today.

Many men have experimented with mail-carrying rockets. Dr. Robert H. Goddard of the United States was conducting experiments as early as 1914. The first successful flight was dispatched in 1931 by Friedrich Schmiedl in Austria. The first American flight took place in 1935. The mail on the various rockets carried labels which were private postage stamps.

While a few experimental rocket mail flights had quasi-postal connections, the first governmental mail that had at least an initial rocket propellant was carried by the American *Apollo XI* astronauts Neil Armstrong and Edwin Aldrin, when they made man's first landing on the moon on July 20, 1969. They carried with them on the moon-landing vehicle *Eagle* an envelope bearing a die proof of a stamp depicting the first step on the moon, made by Armstrong. The envelope was to have been canceled on the moon, but Armstrong and Aldrin were too busy with their experiments, and although this cover, now in the Postal Service archives, does bear a cancel of July 20, 1969, the actual canceling was done aboard *Apollo XI* while it was on the way back to earth. Of course, the envelope and its specially prepared die-proof stamp were in the *Eagle* as it rested on the moon, so it had actually landed on the cancel date.

Armstrong and Aldrin, and Michael Collins, who piloted *Apollo XI* around the moon while Armstrong and Aldrin made the moon landing from *Eagle,* also carried with them the master die (a metal block with the orginal design from which the plate for printing the stamp is made). Once back on earth, after decontamination at Houston's space laboratory, the envelope and the die were given to Postmaster General Winton M. Blount. Blount returned the die to the Bureau of Engraving and Printing, which began processing the commemorative stamp, designed by Paul Calle, for general distribution on September 9, 1969. For this first-day event, stamp collectors from all over the world sent in orders for covers bearing the stamp. These covers were given a double-barreled cancellation—the actual first day of the stamp, September 9, 1969, and below it, the circular-date stamp adapted from the moon-landing cancellation of July 20, 1969. A record 8,743,070 envelopes received the unusual first-day cancellation.

Two years later Postmaster General Blount saw, as did millions of other television viewers, a piece of U.S. mail actually receive a cancellation on the moon. It was made on August 2, 1971, by David Scott, leader of the *Apollo XV* mission. Scott canceled a pair of actual stamps—not a die proof as in the 1969 effort—depicting the "United States in Space/ A Decade of Achievement." The stamps were designed by Robert McCall. Immediately after the event on the moon, which occurred at 8:52 A.M., the pair of stamps went on sale on *terra firma* United States. Only 1,403,-644 covers received a first-day cancellation.

102. Cover with the pair of stamps canceled on the moon during the *Apollo XV* mission in 1971. The faint impression of the cancel was a result of Scott's holding the envelope in one hand while applying the cancel with the other.

IT ALL DEPENDS ON **ZIP CODE** U S 10c

103–7. Among the nations publicizing their ZIP (Zone Improvement Program) postal coding systems has been the United States. The design for the U.S. stamp is adapted from a Randall McDougall Postal Service poster. Also shown are the ZIP stamps of France, China (Formosa), Japan, and South Korea.

103

The Postman Cometh

AT THE TIME OF THE U.S. TAKEOVER of the private New York City local post in 1842, John Lorimer Graham, the New York postmaster, reported to U.S. Postmaster General Charles A. Wickliffe that "the average number of city letters delivered is 437 per day." Such deliveries increased, he later reported, to 762 per day within three months after the absorption by the federal service. He noted that the city mail limits "extend from the Battery to Twenty-second Street, a distance of upwards of three miles, and from the East River to the Hudson, which at some points are distant from each other two miles and a quarter."

In January 1974, John R. Strachan, the New York postmaster, reported that the daily average of mail deposited or in transit through the New York Post Office was 24,871,584 pieces, more than 19,000,000 pieces being first-class mail. In the Manhattan area alone, Mr. Strachan noted that the daily mail delivery was 10,328,458 pieces, more than 8,000,000 being first-class mail.

A means of speeding the mails through the mechanized U.S. system was instituted a decade ago—the ZIP (Zone Improvement Program) code. A number of countries—Great Britain, Canada, India, Formosa, Austria, the Soviet Union, Korea, Japan, for example—have also adopted such a system, which they call "postal coding." Under the system, a series of numbers or letters and numbers are used as part of the forwarding address on all mail. Scanning devices—and, frequently enough, the eyes of a human mail-handler—read these numbers, and drop letters into sacks for a city or for a ZIP- or postal-code zone within a city.

A number of the countries using the postal-code zoning system have issued stamps to publicize the system. The main purpose of these is to alert the individual letter writer. Big users of the mails are required to ZIP-code their product and even sort it by cities before delivery to the post office.

104

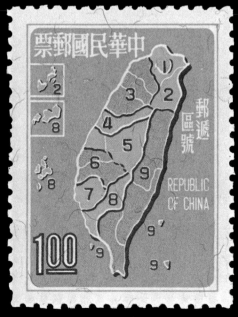

105

106

107

108–110. Four-part stamps of the German states of Mecklenburg-Schwerin and Brunswick, issued in 1856 and 1857, and a Brunswick cover showing three-quarter use.

108

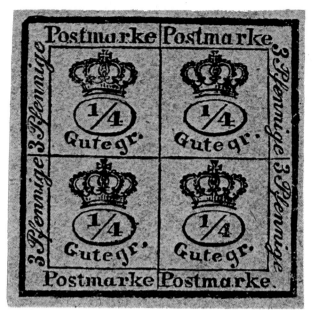

109

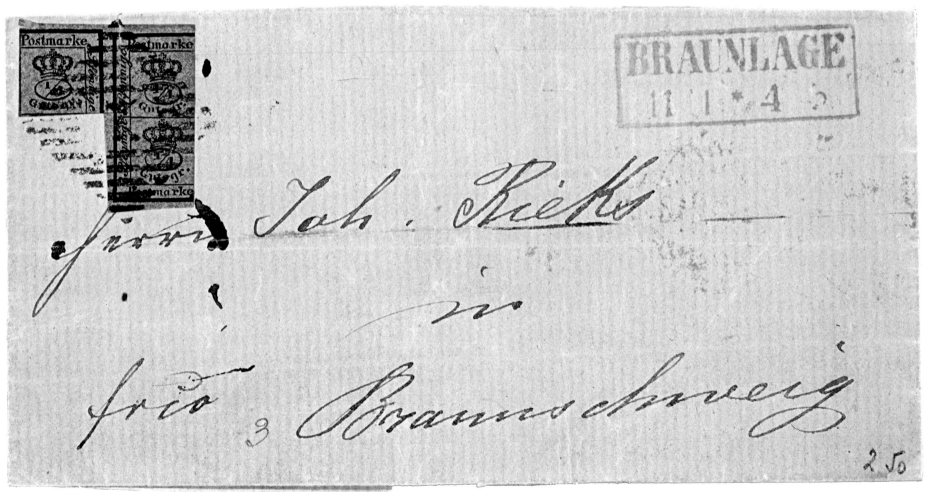

110

111. Cape of Good Hope, Triangle.
First issue, 1853.

Stamps Have Changed, Too

In ELEGANCE, FEW STAMPS have surpassed the skillfully engraved nineteenth-century pioneer Classic stamps. During the first century of postage-stamp design, most followed the style set by the first, the 1840 Penny Black and Two Pence Blue. There were some variations. Among them were triangular stamps from the Cape of Good Hope. Intricacies of postal rates led the German duchies of Mecklenburg-Schwerin and Brunswick to issue four-part single stamps that could be cut into their fourths to make up the necessary postage. In the 1960s and 1970s, strips of stamps—two, three, or four in a row, and blocks of four stamps—were issued by several countries. These were overall pictorials that could be separated by design into single-unit stamps.

The typewriter was utilized in 1895 by a missionary, the Rev. Ernest Millar, to create the first stamps of the British protectorate of Uganda in East Africa. They were used on his and others' correspondence to the outside world. The stamp currency was "cowries," the shells used as coins of barter in the country. Other typewriter stamps have come from the Transvaal during the Boer War; from Siam in 1902; from Albania; and, during World War I, from the Aegean island of Makrónisos in the brief period when, occupied by the British, it was renamed Long Island. Stamps have been overprinted with typewriters to surcharge new denominations. During their occupation of the Ryukyu Islands in World War II, the American marines used the typewriter and a mimeograph machine to provide stamps for the 1945 occupying forces. Ink pads and rubber stamps produced postage stamps in Natal, the republic created by the Boers that is now a province of the Republic of South Africa.

73

112

113

112–15. Four stamps from the United States 1869 issue. The three with inverted centers are among the rarest U.S. stamps. An especially curious effect emanates from the 30c, since its flag is inverted. Although no 90c Lincolns with inverted centers have been discovered, the stamp (right) is among the classic nineteenth-century issues.

114

Although multicolored stamps have become standard today, they were issued only rarely in the nineteenth century. The first bicolored U.S. stamp was issued in 1869. Several rare varieties of it exist in which the centers are printed upside down. Stamps larger than the conventional format did appear in the nineteenth century, usually in a single color.

The Universal Postal Union (U.P.U.) was organized in Berne, Switzerland, in 1874 to promote international postal cooperation. Until that time, individual countries had to make their own arrangements with others for postal exchanges, establishing rates and, by counting each piece of the mail entering, balancing up accounts country by country. The U.P.U. set up a truly international system, fixing rates and encouraging the free flow of correspondence.

In 1897 the world organization resolved that to promote uniformity in the international mails and to simplify the work of sorting clerks certain denominations of stamps should be in the same color: green, generally, for the postal card; red for domestic first-class letters; blue for overseas mail. Other colors were to be used for stamps of higher denominations. One of them, identified as "lake," not a blue or green but a red, was used for some years. Rate structures fluctuated, and over the years the U.P.U. color scheme gradually passed away. The proliferation of multicolored stamps after World War II caused the plan to be abandoned in 1951.

116. German stamps issues of 1921 were in marked contrast to previous staid designs; this plowman was one of several stamps devoted to workmen.

Stamps, a Reflection of Their Times

AT THE TURN OF THE CENTURY there were hints of Art Nouveau in some stamp designs, but the liberation of art styles by the late nineteenth- and early twentieth-century movements did not have a major influence. Today, however, works of art in Impressionist and Art Nouveau styles are frequently reproduced on postage stamps.

Turning through an album of nineteenth-century stamps can be quite uninteresting to the uninitiated: it is a seemingly endless portrait gallery of royalty, presidents, and other rulers. The initiated see the excellence of the portraiture, the fine hand of the men who cut highlights and shadows into metal with infinite accuracy. Engraved stamps, even those a century old, still carry the printed impression of the fine lines of the engraver's burin, a lozenge-shaped steel chisel used to carve recesses in metal that leave lines or dots, forming a picture. There are sometimes minute flaws and errors in the engraving; these are manna to the collector.

After World War I there were some fresh approaches to stamp design. Alphonse Mucha, an Art Nouveau artist, designed some early stamps for his native Czechoslovakia. There were larger-size stamps and new color in France, Germany, Italy, Hungary, and other countries.

At the turn of the twentieth century, United States issues changed from constant portraiture to scenic views and larger stamps, first with a lengthy 1893 series commemorating the Columbian Exposition, then an 1898 group for the Trans-Mississippi Exposition, and then a 1901 series for the Pan-American Exposition. These larger stamps were interspersed with general-issue, or definitive, stamps. Postage stamps began to be message-bearers themselves.

117–19. Netherlands stamps of 1923 and 1924 reflecting the Art Nouveau style.

117

118

119

120

121

122

125

126

127

130

131

132

133

134

135

120–37. To commemorate the World's Columbian Exposition in Chicago in 1893, the United States issued these sixteen stamps, all designed by Alfred Sarony Major. A serious error of color occurred in the 4c, which is blue instead of the intended ultramarine. The normal color is shown in the top strip, the error at the bottom.

123

124

128

129

136

137

138. "Western Cattle in Storm," designed by
Raymond Ostrander Smith, was one of a series of
stamps commemorating the Trans-Mississippi
Exposition in Omaha, Nebraska, in 1898. Smith's
design was based on an engraving by the
Englishman Charles O. Murray after *The Vanguard,*
a painting by John MacWhirter depicting a scene
in the Western Highlands of Scotland.

139. A block of four of a stamp in the Trans-
Mississippi Exposition series, 1898. Designed by
Raymond Ostrander Smith after Frederic
Remington's drawing *Protecting a Wagon Train.*
The block is imperforate horizontally, a rarity.

138

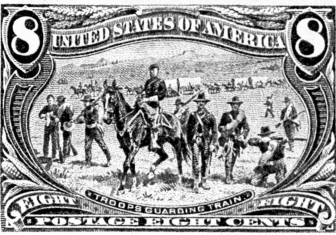

139

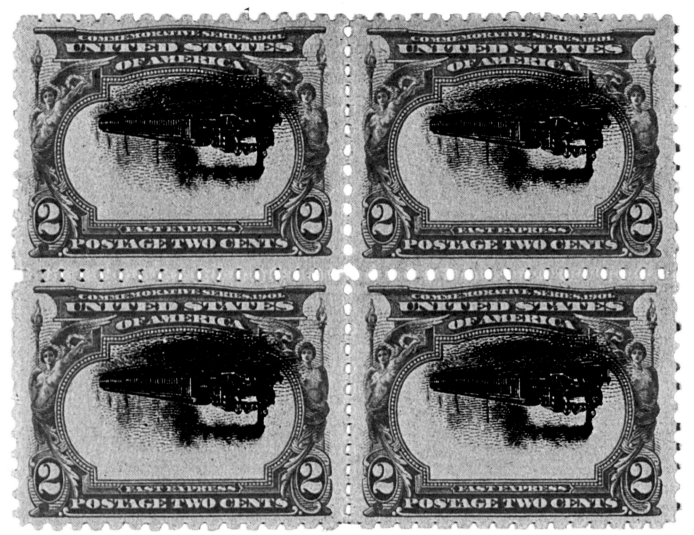

140

141

140, 141. The United States 1901 Pan-American
Exposition issue included a 2c stamp showing
the New York Central Railroad's "Empire
State Express" and a 4c showing the
Baltimore & Ohio Railroad's electric
automobile. Both were designed by Raymond
Ostrander Smith. The block of four of the 2c
with the center inverted is unique.

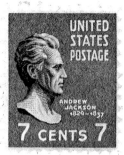

142. A stamp in the 1938–43 United States presidential series, portraying Andrew Jackson. Elaine Rawlinson supplied the basic design for the series, which was issued in values ranging from 1/2c through $5.00.

143. The first nonpictorial United States stamp, commemorating the opening sessions of the United Nations at San Francisco in 1945. Designed by Victor S. McCloskey, Jr.

144. James Stoddert's 1718 map of the region around Annapolis was the basis for this design by Charles R. Chickering for the tercentenary (1949) of the settlement of the Maryland capital.

145. World War II postal remembrances include this 1948 tribute to Gold Star Mothers—those who lost sons in the war.

The years between the two world wars brought changes in postage-stamp patterns, a notable event being the 1938–43 presidential series, with values ranging from half-cent to $5.00, in which medallion portraits of the presidents through Calvin Coolidge were etched in. The appearance was based on a prize-winning design by Elaine Rawlinson.

The death of Franklin D. Roosevelt, himself a stamp collector, inspired nothing more than bank-note dull memorial stamps, but shortly before his death the president had approved the first nonpictorial U.S. stamp to commemorate the opening, two weeks later, of the inaugural United Nations sessions in San Francisco. It was a simple arrangement of four lines of type, "Toward/United Nations/April 25, 1945," with his name below. (The United Nations began to issue its own stamps in 1951.)

New issues that followed included a commemorative for the frigate *Constitution*, a tribute to Gold Star Mothers, stamps memorializing Lincoln's Gettysburg Address, the tercentenary of the settlement of Annapolis, the centennial of Commodore Matthew C. Perry's visit to Japan, the tercentenary of New York City's settlement, the Battle of Fort Ticonderoga, and a stamp honoring American architects.

Multicolored stamps began with an issue showing the whooping crane and urging wildlife conservation. There was an American Credo series with inspiring words from Washington, Franklin, Jefferson, Francis Scott Key, Lincoln, and Patrick Henry. There were statehood stamps for Kansas, New Mexico, Louisiana, and Arizona; a commemorative honoring the nursing profession; a stamp for John H. Glenn's 1962 orbital flight in space; and stamps commemorating Food for Peace, Sam Houston, homemakers, Winston Churchill, the circus, Henry David Thoreau, Walt Disney, Daniel Boone, Sidney Lanier, the 1972 Olympic Games, and Christmas.

Paintings by American artists appeared on U.S. stamps: the works of Frederic Remington, Winslow Homer, John James Audubon, Charles M. Russell, Stuart Davis, Mary Cassatt, Thomas Eakins, John Trumbull, Grandma Moses, Edward Hopper, and others.

In 1953 postal officials formed the Citizens' Stamp Advisory Committee, a group of artists, historians, graphics technicians, and stamp collectors who brought living American artists into the design of U.S. stamps. Among these have been Norman Rockwell, Stevan Dohanos, Arnold Copeland, Leonard Baskin, Robert Greissman, Bradbury Thompson, Frank Conley, Rudolph Wendelin, Douglas Gorsline, George Samerjan, Antonio Frasconi, Sam Marsh, the cartoonist Herbert Block ("Herblock"), Ward Brackett, Norman Todhunter, Leon Helguera, John Maass, Gyo Fujikawa, William H. Buckley, Robert W. Hines, and Peter Max.

146. Patrick Henry's defiance of George III as colonial Americans debated their allegiance to their mother country inspired this design by Frank Conley, one of a series of six American Credo stamps of 1960–61. Quotations from George Washington, Benjamin Franklin, Thomas Jefferson, Francis Scott Key, and Abraham Lincoln were also used in the series.

147. For one hundred years of Kansas statehood, 1961.

148. Norman Todhunter's design commemorating the 1962 sesquicentennial of Louisiana statehood shows a Mississippi riverboat passing a moss-hung tree.

149. This 1961 salute to nursing was designed by Alfred Charles Parker.

150. A combination of lithography and letterpress printing was used in this 1964 issue to produce a sampler effect. The stamp, showing an American farm couple in front of their house, was designed by Norman Todhunter to commemorate the fiftieth anniversary of the establishment of an extension educational service of the U.S. Department of Agriculture aimed at improving home life. The lithographed background provided a clothlike "surface" for the color engraving.

151. Edward Klauck's 1966 stamp commemorating a century of the circus in America.

152. To commemorate the 150th anniversary of the birth of Henry David Thoreau, Leonard Baskin adapted this portrait from an 1845 daguerreotype of the essayist.

153. Ervine Metzl's design for this 1959 commemorative of the sesquicentennial of Lincoln's birth was based on a drawing by Fritz Busse of the head of Abraham Lincoln from the Daniel Chester French statue in the Lincoln Memorial in Washington, D.C.

154–56. Three United States revenue stamps—$5.00, $200.00, and $500.00. Black-and-white reproduction does not do justice to these stamps, especially the $500.00, known as the "Persian rug" partly because of its proportions (almost four inches tall and slightly more than two inches wide) but chiefly because of its multicolored design.

157

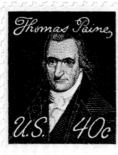

158

159

160

161

162

163

164

165

166

157. Charles R. Chickering's 1954 design commemorating the sesquicentennial of the expedition of Meriwether Lewis and William Clark into the Louisiana Territory includes Sacagawea, the Indian maiden who befriended and accompanied the explorers. The figures of Lewis and Clark are based on a statue by Charles Keck in Charlottesville, Va.; that of Sacagawea is adapted from a statue by Leonard Crunkle in Bismark, N.D.

158. The philosopher Thomas Paine, whose 1776 pamphlet, *Common Sense*, urged immediate declaration of American independence, is pictured on this 1968 stamp. Robert Geissmann's design was based on a portrait by John Wesley Jarvis.

159. Norman Rockwell's design for the 1963 centenary of city mail delivery supplied the first touch of humor on a U.S. stamp.

160. Early in the nineteenth century, John Chapman, an eccentric nurseryman, planted apple seeds throughout the countryside of Pennsylvania, Ohio, and Indiana, thus earning the nickname "Johnny Appleseed." He is shown here on Robert Bode's 1966 stamp.

161. Lucy Stone, a nineteenth-century pioneer advocate of women's rights, depicted by Mark English in this 1968 issue. She used her maiden name throughout her career, even after her marriage to Dr. Henry Blackwell.

162. David K. Stone's 1970 stamp commemorating the 150th anniversary of Fort Snelling. The fort, located on a bluff south of Minneapolis at the junction of the Mississippi and Minnesota rivers, was no log cabin, but a vast sandstone complex, the center of military and social affairs in the Northwest Territory.

163. A 10c stamp from a 1913 Panama-Pacific Exposition series. Its orange color, deeper than the orange-yellow of most stamps in the issue, gives it increased value.

164. Someone in the Post Office apparently believed the myth that Betsy Ross created the United States flag, for in 1952 this stamp, based on a painting by C. H. Weisgerber, was issued to commemorate the 200th anniversary of the seamstress's birth. George Washington, Robert Morris, and George Ross, a relative of Mrs. Ross, are pictured.

165. This 1863 stamp portraying Andrew Jackson, known to stamp collectors as the "Black Jack," is the dominant portrait stamp of U.S. nineteenth-century issues. Designed by James McDonnough after a miniature by John Wood Dodge.

166. Mark Twain's tale of Tom Sawyer is recalled in this design by Norman Rockwell adapted for this 1972 stamp from one of his illustrations for a 1937 Heritage Club edition.

170

167

Because many United States stamps and stamped envelopes were in the possession of Confederate postmasters during the early stages of the Civil War, the federal government decreed that stamps issued prior to the start of the conflict were no longer valid for postage. These were the only U.S. stamps ever demonetized. However, some southerners did use the federal issues, resulting in these rare covers.

167. A cover from Charleston, South Carolina, with "Southn Letter/ Unpaid," one of the rarest markings. The stamped envelope is from a U.S. 1860 issue; the marking "Paid 10" represents the Confederate fee for the New York distance. The "Due 3" marking indicates that the "Paid 10" was ignored, and that the federal postmaster required the postage due before delivery.

168. An 1861 cover from New Orleans. The marking "Cannot be forwarded" indicates that there was no mail service to Marshall, Texas.

During the Civil War, many local Confederate postmasters issued their own stamps; the infrequent use of these postmaster provisionals has made them among the rarest of American issues.

169. A cover from Charleston, South Carolina, with the local postmaster's lithographed 5c blue provisional. 1861.

170. The Mobile, Alabama, 2c black lithographed star. The Mobile postmaster also issued a lithographed 5c blue. 1861.

171. Letterpress-printed 5c provisional from Pleasant Shade, Virginia. 1861.

172. One of the rarest of the Confederate States general issues, a block of four of the 1863 "frame-line" Jefferson Davis. The stamps were printed by Archer and Daly of Richmond, Virginia.

171

168

169

172

Abroad, numerous changes have come in the designing of stamps. Staid Great Britain has broken out stamps in many hues, upsetting a century-old tradition of line-engraved portraits of royalty, with stamps honoring Winston Churchill, Robert Burns, and—its first stamp-portrait of a foreigner—Mahatma Gandhi. Stamps of the dominions have also changed.

Handsome emissions have come from France, Austria, Belgium, the German Federal Republic, Sweden, Portugal, Ireland, and occasionally from Spain, Italy, Finland, Denmark, and the Netherlands.

Russia's stamps have honored numerous domestic heroes as well as some foreigners. Americans so honored have included such disparate figures as William Z. Foster, Benjamin Franklin, Henry W. Longfellow, Samuel L. Clemens, and William Henry Porter ("O. Henry"). Among famous men and women of other nationalities honored have been Shakespeare, Darwin, William Blake, Gandhi, Rabindranath Tagore, and Selma Lagerlöf. Surprisingly, there have been Russian stamps with religious themes, generally Madonnas adapted from famous paintings in the Hermitage and other Russian museums. Russia has also postally honored notables of Estonia, Latvia, and Lithuania.

In Asia, Japan has issued colorful postage stamps, as have the former French Indochina states—Vietnam (North and South), Laos, and Cambodia—and Indonesia. Some impressive issues have come from Formosa (Republic of China) as well as the People's Republic of China (mainland). For almost a quarter of a century the sale of stamps of mainland China was prohibited in the U.S., but the ban was dropped after President Nixon's visit there in 1972.

During the occupation of Germany after World War II, the Allied zones of control maintained their own postal facilities and issued their own postage stamps. The same was done by the Allied Military Government in Italy, the German "General Gouvernement" in Poland during the war, and the Japanese in their occupied territories.

THE THIRTY YEARS that followed issuance of the first postage stamps in 1840 brought forth stamps from about 140 countries, large and small. About half of these are now incorporated into larger nations. Zurich, Geneva, and Basel, which were the second states to issue their own stamps, ceased to exist in 1850; stamps after that date were issued by the country of Switzerland. Bavaria, Saxony, Prussia, Hanover, Baden, and other German states that are now parts of East or West Germany also issued stamps.

Victoria, Queensland, New South Wales, Tasmania, and other districts of Australia once issued their own stamps, as did Sardinia, Tuscany, Modena, Parma, Naples, Romagna, and Sicily, now part of the republic of Italy. The provinces of Canada that once issued stamps ceased their emissions at the time of confederation in 1867. Serbia, Montenegro, the Hawaiian Islands, the Cape of Good Hope, Natal, Shanghai, and a host of other nineteenth-century stamp-issuing entities are now part of larger domains.

The old states produced many of the world's Classic stamps in that thirty-year period. Although they are no longer nations, their names live on in stamp catalogues and albums. Replacing these have been the many new states created from the former colonial empires of Great Britain, France, the Netherlands, Germany, and Belgium.

Where in the first thirty years of postage stamps there had been about 140 stamp-issuing states, there are now more than 250. The nations of the world are proliferating. Only a few hundred stamps were produced yearly; now more than 6,000 new stamps are issued each year.

A high proportion of these new stamps are issued by new nations.

Proliferation of Nations and Stamps

174

175

176

177

174–76. The first stamps of Switzerland. *left to right*: canton of Zurich, 1843; the "double Geneva," canton of Geneva, 1843; the Basel "Dove," canton of Basel, 1845.

177. W. B. Perot, the postmaster at Hamilton, Bermuda, in 1848, provided a mailbox outside his home for the deposit of letters. Patrons were supposed to include a penny for postage. When some of them failed to do this, Perot made this stamp and sold it to them. Fewer than a dozen of these stamps have survived.

178. France, first issue, 1849.

179. Bavaria, first issue, 1849.

180. New South Wales, Sydney View, 1850. The first pictorial stamp.

181. Spain, first issue, 1850. Portrait of Isabella II.

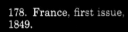

182

183

182, 183. Victoria, first issue, 1850. Two rare stamps with portrait of Queen Victoria.

184, 185. Nova Scotia and
New Brunswick, 1851. Early
diamond-shaped stamps.

184

186

186. Canada, first issue, 1851.
One of the world's rarest
stamps.

185

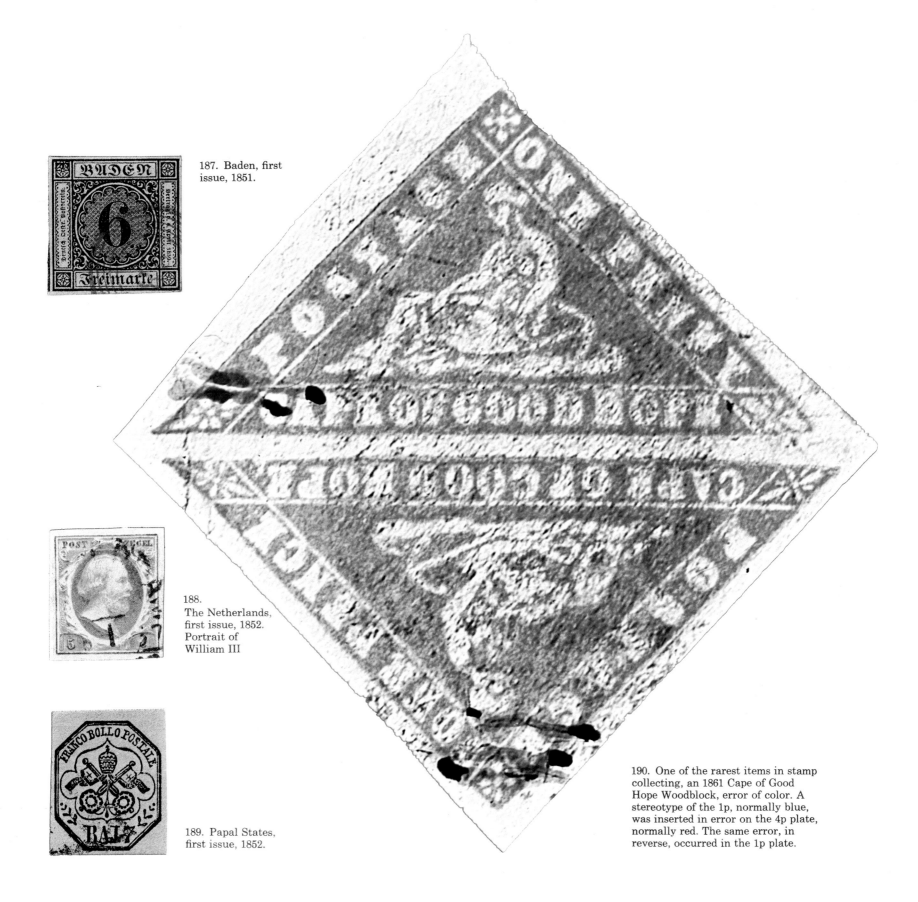

187. Baden, first issue, 1851.

188. The Netherlands, first issue, 1852. Portrait of William III

189. Papal States, first issue, 1852.

190. One of the rarest items in stamp collecting, an 1861 Cape of Good Hope Woodblock, error of color. A stereotype of the 1p, normally blue, was inserted in error on the 4p plate, normally red. The same error, in reverse, occurred in the 1p plate.

191. Van Diemen's Land (now Tasmania), first issue, 1853. Portrait of Queen Victoria.

192. The unique Sweden error of color, from the country's first issue, 1855. The 3-skilling banco appeared in orange instead of the normal blue-green.

191

192

193

193, 194. Western Australia, Black Swan. First issue, 1854. *above*: as reproduced on the 1954 centenary commemorative.

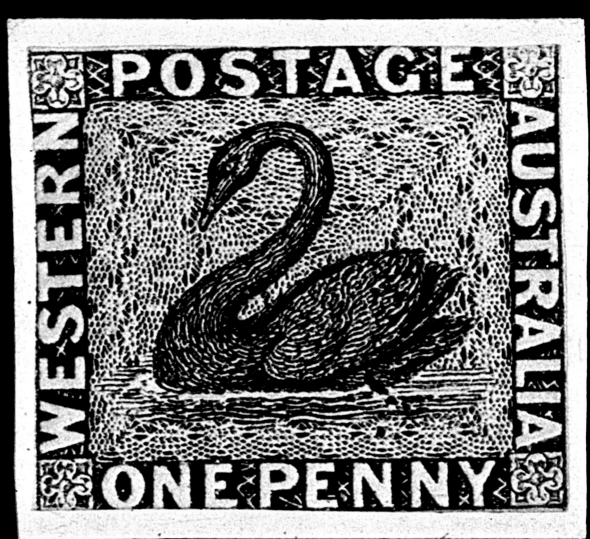

194

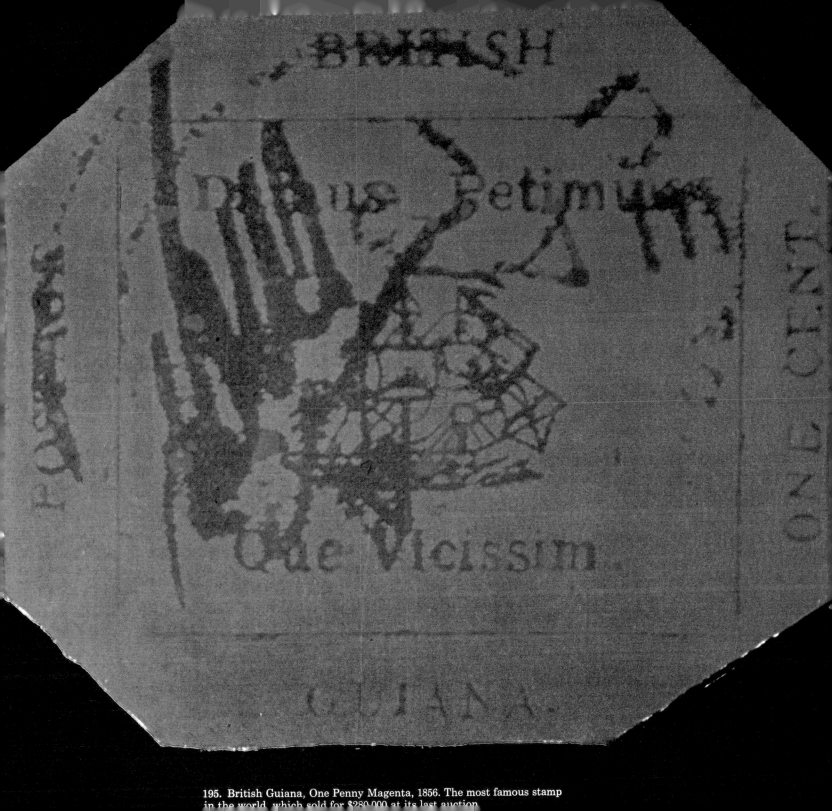

195. British Guiana, One Penny Magenta, 1856. The most famous stamp
in the world, which sold for $280,000 at its last auction.

196. Finland, first issue, 1856. Coat of arms of Finland.

197. Newfoundland, first issue (triangular type), 1857.

198. Rumania's first stamps, issued in 1858, were from the principality of Moldavia and showed bull's heads. The 81 parales is the rarest, shown here *tête-bêche* with a 27 parales.

199. Austria, 1863. Early stamp of the coat-of-arms type featuring embossing.

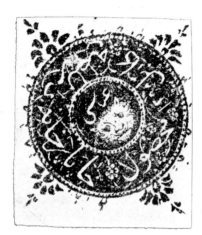

200. Afghanistan, first issue, 1871. Tiger's-head center design, apparently honoring the contemporary amir, Sher ("Tiger") Ali.

201. To commemorate the opening in 1959 of the St. Lawrence Seaway between Canada and the United States, both countries issued stamps of identical design showing a maple leaf and an American eagle. In the Canadian issue some of the centers were inverted—one of the few flaws discovered in Canadian stamps.

202. Gambia, 1869. Outstanding for its cameo-like portrait of Queen Victoria.

Pakistan came from the partition of India, and out of Pakistan came Bangladesh. Ceylon became a republic and reverted to an ancient name, Sri Lanka, and the Republic of Indonesia was born out of the old Netherlands East Indies. In Africa, Bechuanaland became Botswana, Burundi came from the old Belgian Africa, the Gold Coast became Ghana. The country of Lesotho was formerly Basutoland; Zaire was formerly part of the Belgian Congo. Madagascar has become the Malagasy Republic, Nyasaland is now Malawi, Mali is the old Sudanese Republic, and Tanzania was formed by the union of Tanganyika and Zanzibar.

In the New World, British Guiana became Guyana and British Honduras, Belize.

All these new nations and many more have issued postage stamps, but as a stamp-issuing entity one source is unsurpassed: the United Nations.

Following World War I and the formation of the League of Nations, with headquarters in Switzerland, Swiss stamps for use by the league were overprinted "Société des Nations." These overprints are forerunners of today's United Nations stamps.

In the infancy of the U.N., following its beginning in San Francisco in 1945, some delegates urged that the organization establish its own postal facilities. After many months of discussion, which involved U.S. postal officials and, as advisers to the U.N., postal officials of other countries, an accord was reached. Briefly, the agreement was that the U.S. would operate the postal facilities at the U.N. headquarters in New York City, and would be compensated for servicing mail emanating from the U.N. The U.N. Postal Administration would issue stamps, retaining for itself only the moneys obtained through the sale of its stamps to collectors.

The U.N., pioneering in the establishment of an advisory committee to counsel its postal administration on stamp design, issued its first stamps in 1951. In the years since, the U.N. stamps have been among the world's most attractive postal emissions. They are created by artists and printers in many countries, and generally bear the name of the organization in the five official languages—English, French, Spanish, Russian, and Chinese.

The only U.N. stamps validated for use are those which emanate from the headquarters building in New York or from the organization's European headquarters in Geneva.

203, 204. For thirty-five years, 1903–38, The Sower (*La Semeuse*) was the basic design on French stamps. The figure was adapted from a French coin by the medalist Louis Oscar Roty. The stamp on the left was used continuously during this period: it appeared in dozens of denominations with backgrounds in a great variety of colors. The one on the right, including the ground under the sower's feet, had a short life; it was issued only in 1906.

Gimmickry

A DISTURBING ELEMENT in the increasing number of stamp-issuing countries and the sharp rise in the number of stamps issued yearly is the number of unnecessary stamps that are produced. Many nations, mostly small ones, issue stamps for which there is no real need. Stamp collectors are prone to buy almost anything that appears on the market, and promotion-minded postal officials and entrepreneurs reap a goodly reward from this tendency, usually in countries other than the issuing one.

The chief offenders have been the new African states and the sheikdoms bordering the Persian Gulf. In the 1960s these countries issued innumerable postage stamps, all official; few ever saw their own homelands.

Entrepreneurs, home-based or in the U.S. or Europe, have had stamps produced at various security-printers in Austria, Britain, and other countries with the support of local postal administrations. They forward some of the products to the home country to make them official, then distribute the remainder to dealers throughout the world. The stamps, usually multicolored, are frequently quite beautiful and often feature popular subjects—works of art, authors, flowers, birds—that interest the growing number of "topical stamp" collectors, those who collect by the subject of a stamp's design.

The entrepreneurs have not been content with a few denominations for normal needs: they have plunged the collector into long sets, six or eight stamps, including high denominations for which, even in more sophisticated countries, there is only a limited need. These sets have brought the promoters $5.00 to $7.00 for a set which costs pennies to produce and doesn't require postal servicing.

Stamps flowed during the 1960s from such places as Fujeira, Sharjah, Ajman, Umm al Qain, Raz al Khaimina, and the "State of Oman," which did not exist except in the minds of some dissidents in Muscat and Oman. More recently, the Persian Gulf States have merged into the "United Arab Emirates," and the flow of stamps has diminished.

Not all the sinners have been tiny nations: some major states get into the act. Russia, for example, issues a great many stamps each year.

(The country has not provided statistics, so the exact number is unknown.) These often end up in "collectors' packets"—original stamps, gum intact, some of them canceled to order.

The United States issues about twenty to forty stamps a year. The Postal Service has estimated that there are about 16,000,000 stamp collectors in the U.S., most of them, it is believed, collecting the stamps of their own country. Even with a printing of 150,000,000 stamps of a single issue, many collectors desire not only a single stamp but what are called "plate-number blocks" (stamps plus the printers' numbers that appear in the selvedge on the pane of stamps); an indication of how many stamps must go into stamp albums. Once these plate-number blocks had a single number, or perhaps two, and were collected in blocks of four with an occasional block of six stamps. Now panes are appearing with six or more plate numbers and all sorts of collectible units, such as the slogan "Mail Early in the Day" or the "Mr. Zip" insignia. When there are six plate numbers, it means they have to be in a block which would be two stamps wide, six stamps deep—twelve stamps to be purchased, not four.

In 1969 the British General Post Office became a public corporation. At that time it surrendered stamp-issuing authority to several small island communities. There were two new issuers that year—the English Channel islands of Guernsey and Jersey. The bailiwick of Guernsey includes the islands of Alderney, Sark, Herm, Jethou, and Lithou. In July 1973 the Isle of Man in the Irish Sea was granted permission to issue its own stamps. Although there is no need for any of these island dependencies to issue stamps at all—they are still part of the United Kingdom—such stamps are an effective way of producing revenue.

France issues about forty stamps annually, and Canada about the same number. There have been remarks about Liechtenstein and Luxembourg living off their numerous stamps; actually both issue only a limited number of stamps each year. Monaco, however, does seem to issue more stamps than it requires.

Then there are the countries that jump onto almost any bandwagon. The quadrennial Olympic Games have been a natural reason for participating nations to issue stamps, but why are Winter Olympic stamps issued by the African states or by nations that are not even members of the International Olympic Committee and do not participate in the games?

Any nation may, of course, honor men and women of other nations on its postage stamps. A number took postal note of the assassination of John F. Kennedy, and some African countries have issued matching stamps of Lenin and Franklin D. Roosevelt. Abraham Lincoln, Winston Churchill, Mahatma Gandhi, Charles de Gaulle, and Pope John XXIII are among many others who have been commemorated.

205–7. Kurt Plowitz's triptych of children in a play train, issued by the United Nations in 1966 to commemorate the twentieth anniversary of UNICEF (the United Nations International Children's Emergency Fund).

Propaganda

THE POSTAGE STAMP HAS BECOME a prime tool for propaganda, used to promote peace, argue for human rights, warn against drugs, urge the eradication of diseases, seek aid for refugees, children, and the aged, and support for the arts. Many stamps issued for these reasons are classified as "semi-postals," that is, stamps displaying two denominations, one for the actual carriage of the letter, the other, usually smaller, for funds contributed to the cause.

Stamps are used to promote the sale of a nation's products and recommend tourist sites or attractions. They note good will between nations, promote the idea of a European community, solicit funds for the World Health Organization, and caution against highway accidents. They promote the protection and preservation of natural resources. Stamps have been used in countries turning their traffic from left lanes to right to remind people of the change.

They have been used for espionage, too. Stories are told of spies using stamps on mail to tell of the movements of ships and troops, and to conceal microfilm. During World War I, American and British counter-intelligence agents forged German, Austrian, and Bavarian stamps to disseminate propaganda, and the practice was repeated in World War II.

During that war the British forged German stamps to mail letters within Germany to widows of soldiers warning them that if their behavior was not exemplary—Hitler would be the judge—they would be considered divorced and lose their widow's pensions. Among the forged Allied stamps was one displaying a skeletal head of Hitler and one of his Gestapo chief, Heinrich Himmler. These are thought to have been dropped over Germany by British planes during an air raid.

HALT! RAUSCHGIFT IST SELBSTMORD

2S

REPUBLIK ÖSTERREICH

O. STEFFERL   1973

208. The eradication of drug abuse is the subject of this 1973 Austrian stamp by Otto Stefferl.

FLYKTING 71

SVERIGE 55

ALF OLSSON del.   1971   CZ. SLANIA sc.

209. Alf Olsson's Swedish stamp of 1971 is one of many which have taken refugees and their plight as their subject.

TO LIVE TOGETHER ANOTHER *
WITH ONE IN PEACE

UNITED NATIONS 聯合國
ОБЪЕДИНЕННЫЕ НАЦИИ
NACIONES UNIDAS
NATIONS UNIES   1c

210. Kurt Plowitz's 1962 United Nations stamp, "To Live Together in Peace with One Another."

PORTUGAL 9.00

mês internacional
do coração

ANTÓNIO GARCIA - DES.   LITO. DE PORTUGAL

211. In 1972, many countries issued stamps promoting Heart Month. The above, designed by Antonio Garcia, is from Portugal.

PRO PATRIA 1971

HELVETIA 20+10

JEAN PRAHIN   COURVOISIER S.A.

212. Switzerland issues annual National Day stamps with plus denominations. In this 1971 stamp depicting a cockerel, the designer, Jean Prahin, achieved a stained-glass effect.

1953 1963

Dix Ans de Protection Européenne des Droits de L'Homme

2,50F

LUXEMBOURG

ENSCHEDÉ · HOLLAND   S.L.HARTZ

213

PAPUA & NEW GUINEA

HUMAN RIGHTS YEAR

5c

214

PAPUA & NEW GUINEA

HUMAN RIGHTS YEAR

10c

215

PAPUA & NEW GUINEA

UNIVERSAL SUFFRAGE

25c

216

5c

DR. HILDA BYNOE, GOVERNOR

EIIR

HUMAN RIGHTS YEAR 1968

GRENADA

217

2D

1968

MALTA

INTERNATIONAL YEAR FOR HUMAN RIGHTS

218

HAK² MANUSIA
DROITS DE L'HOMME   15 sen

IO-XII
1948
1958

REPUBLIK
INDONESIA

219

NACIONES UNIDAS   聯合國   3c

HUMAN RIGHTS
DROITS DE L'HOMME
DERECHOS HUMANOS
IO.XII.1948-57   ПРАВА ЧЕЛОВЕКА   人權

ОБЪЕДИНЕННЫЕ НАЦИИ

UNITED NATIONS   NATIONS UNIES

220

UNITED NATIONS

NACIONES UNIDAS   聯合國   ОБЪЕДИНЕННЫЕ НАЦИИ

IO-XII   1948-54

HUMAN RIGHTS 人權   3c
DERECHOS HUMANOS
3c   ПРАВА ЧЕЛОВЕКА
DROITS DE L'HOMME

NATIONS UNIES

221

1.00

世界人權宣言
十週年紀念

中華民國郵票

222

Human rights has been the subject of numerous stamps, many linked to the Universal Declaration of Human Rights of the United Nations, December 10, 1948.

213. The tenth anniversary of the European Convention of Human Rights was marked by Luxembourg with this 1963 stamp by Sem Hartz showing twelve stars symbolic of the Council of Europe.

214–16. Human Rights and Universal Suffrage are the subjects of these 1968 stamps issued by Papua New Guinea. Designed by George Hamori.

217. Gov. Hilda Bynoe's portrait is featured on a 1969 Grenada stamp.

218. Malta's 1968 Human Rights stamp, designed by E. V. Cremona.

219. One of Indonesia's five 1958 postal commemoratives of the Declaration. Designed by Junalies.

220, 221. Two examples of the annual Human Rights Day stamps issued by the United Nations: Leonard Mitchell designed the 1954 stamp showing the mother and child, and Olav Mathiesen designed the 1957 stamp with the flaming torch.

222. China (Formosa) in 1958 issued this stamp designed by Wen Hsueh-yu showing a globe encircled by a flame from a torch of liberty.

Friendship between nations is occasionally marked by stamps, as is enmity.

223. Russia's Friendship House in Moscow appeared on this 1962 issue.

224, 225. Identical stamps issued in 1973 by France and West Germany to mark the accord that has developed between the two countries since World War II.

226. Norway, a signatory to an Antarctic treaty pledging nonmilitarization of the Antarctic continent, issued this stamp in 1971 to commemorate the treaty's tenth anniversary.

227. This Egyptian stamp, symbolizing the stresses in the Middle East, was issued in 1973, a few weeks after an Israeli jet shot down a Libyan airliner, resulting in heavy loss of life.

228. South Korean stamp of 1972 commemorating a meeting between its Red Cross organization and that of North Korea.

223

227

224

225

228

226

229. 1956, Daniel Gonzaque,
France

230. 1957, Werner Weiskönig,
Switzerland

231. 1957, Richard Blank, German Federal Republic

European unity, exemplified by the Common Market, is carried on by postmen of the Conférence Européenne des Administrations des Postes et des Télécommunications—CEPT, a confederation of postal and telegraph-telephone administrations. The expansion of the six nations of the European Coal and Steel Community into a broader community was forecast in the Europa stamps, issued in 1956. CEPT was born in 1959 and took up the idea of postal unity. From 1959 through 1973, most of the member nations used a universal stamp design for an annual commemoration of the Europa concept. European artists competed to create the yearly design, which reflected the growth of CEPT from nineteen charter members, represented by the nineteen-spoke wheel of 1960, to its present twenty-six members.

The current membership of CEPT includes Austria, Belgium, Denmark, Cyprus, Finland, France (including Andorra), Germany, Great Britain, Greece, Iceland, Ireland, Italy, Liechtenstein, Luxembourg, Malta, Monaco, The Netherlands, Norway, Portugal, San Marino, Spain, Sweden, Switzerland, Turkey, Vatican City, and Yugoslavia.

232. Italy commemorated the twentieth anniversary of the European Coal and Steel Community—France, Germany, Italy, The Netherlands, Belgium, and Luxembourg—with this 1971 stamp honoring its founders, Konrad Adenauer of West Germany, Robert Schuman of France, and Alcide de Gasperi of Italy.

233, 234. Great Britain and Ireland entered the Common Market in 1973, noting the event with these stamps. The British interlocking jig-saw design is by P. Murdoch. The Irish stamp, by Louis le Brocquy, depicts the Celtic head motif—there are 434—a symbol of unity.

232

233

234

235. 1958, André van
der Vossen, The Netherlands

236. 1959, Walter Brudi,
German Federal Republic

237. 1960, Pentti Rahikainen,
Finland

238. 1961, Theo Kurpershoek,
The Netherlands

239. 1962, Lex Weyer, Luxembourg

240. 1963, Arne Holm, Norway

241. 1964, Georges Betemps,
France

242. 1965, Hardur Karlsson, Iceland

243. 1966, Gregor and
Joseph Bender, German
Federal Republic

245. 1968, Hans Schwarzenbach,
Switzerland

246. 1969, Luigi Gasbarra and
Giorgio Belli, Italy

244. 1967, Oscar Bonnevalle,
Belgium

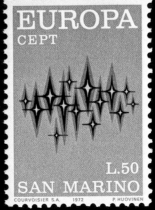

251–57. Safety in the home and on the highways has been the subject for numerous propaganda stamps. A 1971 stamp issued by West Germany cautioned children against playing with matches. Belgium (1972) and Syria (1971) called attention to road signs and traffic signals. Czechoslovakia showed a cloverleaf turnoff from a throughway on a 1971 pair. Norway (1969) called attention to children crossing streets. Poland (1969) cautioned pedestrians to keep to the left side of the road, and Sweden took note (1967) of its changed rule of the road—to keep to the right.

The Germans instituted a countermove with parodies of British stamps. These were the work of a group of engravers and printers who were Jewish prisoners at the Sachsenhausen concentration camp. One such parody was of the 1935 King George V Silver Jubilee issue in which the king's portrait was replaced by one of Josef Stalin. The title, Silver Jubilee Halfpenny, was changed to the slogan "This is a Jewsh [sic] War," with the Star of David and the Hammer and Sickle added. Another was a satire of a 1937 stamp commemorating the coronation of George VI, bearing his portrait and that of Queen Elizabeth. Stalin's portrait replaced that of the queen, titles were changed, and "Teheran-28.11.1943" replaced the coronation date of 12 May 1937, implying that Russia had gained concessions from Britain at the Teheran Conference.

Other stamps from Germany alleged British perfidy in bombings and were overprinted with such slogans as "England bleeds on the order of Moscow." There was a long series of forgeries of various British colony stamps with the overprint "Liquidation of Empire." All these forgeries are still in existence. So-called used copies of these forgeries also exist, but we have no proof that they were actually used on mail. They could have been created from fake canceling devices.

More recently, in the 1950s, North Korea counterfeited U.S. stamps to mail propaganda into South Korea. During the American presence in Vietnam, North Vietnam on several occasions released stamps—not forgeries—charging the U.S. with atrocities or claiming the shooting-down of large numbers of American planes. Cuba and East Germany issued anti-American stamps as propaganda during the Vietnam War.

Other political propaganda efforts made with stamps have included the distribution in 1900 to American Congressmen of a Nicaraguan stamp showing an erupting volcano (Mount Monotombo) in that country during discussions then in progress about the digging of a trans-Isthmian canal. Argentina has issued several stamps proclaiming her right to the Falkland Islands (Islas Malvinas), a group of British-occupied islands off her coast in the South Atlantic.

STAMPS ARE GOVERNMENT BUSINESS, of course; they are also a commercial trade product.

Operating a post office is not profitable. Benjamin Franklin was the last American postmaster general to show a profit—when he was a colonial official for George III. Today, almost every postal administration throughout the world is in "trade," the business of providing too many stamps, first-day covers, and quite a few gimcracks, frequently interesting but not always worthwhile.

The U.S. Post Office Department in 1921 went into the business of selling stamps to stamp collectors from selected stocks, well-centered stamps in which the design has a uniform white perforated edge. Major post offices in the U.S. have had special "philatelic windows" selling this type of stamp for years, and the Post Office has maintained its philatelic sales service in Washington for more than half a century. When, some years ago, it attempted to economize by closing down the service, the resulting complaints from stamp collectors caused it to change its mind. The Post Office Department was succeeded in 1971 by the U.S. Postal Service, which still provides a service to collectors desiring first-day cancellations.

The philatelic windows have now become "postiques" that sell Postal Service products such as an excellent catalogue of U.S. stamps, posters, cards, packets of stamps, and beginners' collections that include foreign stamps. The postiques provide the stamp collector with an opportunity to help the Postal Service reduce its deficits. Most governments offer the same services. Some postal administrations have acquired private sales agencies to promote and sell their wares, which has led to promotions pressing for more stamps.

The U.S. Postal Service is the brainchild of former Postmaster General Lawrence F. O'Brien, who suggested in 1967 that the Post Office should be given rate-making privileges (previously a prerogative of Congress) which would enable it to operate as a business paying its own way rather than as a tax-supported enterprise. Higher postal rates have resulted, but the deficits continue.

It's a Business, Too

Printers

THE PRODUCTION OF POSTAGE STAMPS is government business, but the stamp-printing business is not always governmental. Many countries operate security-printing establishments that produce their stamps, securities, and paper currency. Among these are the United States, France, Austria, Japan, Belgium, Italy, West Germany, Spain, Denmark, Norway, Sweden, Portugal, India, Egypt, Ireland, Mexico, Argentina, Brazil, the Iron Curtain countries, and others.

Private printers produce postage stamps for Great Britain, Canada, the Netherlands, Greece, Israel, Finland, the independent nations that emerged from the former British, French, Dutch, and Belgian empires, and many other nations.

Some governments, notably Austria and Japan, compete with commercial houses in printing stamps for other countries. The U.S. Bureau of Engraving and Printing provides stamps for the Canal Zone and did so for the Philippine Islands until the latter became independent in 1946. Hungary has been printing the stamps of Mongolia for some years and acts as Mongolia's press and sales agent. United Nations stamps have been produced by private firms as well as some government printers in many countries, including Great Britain, the United States, Canada, Japan, Switzerland, Austria, Czechoslovakia, West Germany, Spain, Finland, Greece, and Turkey.

The first United States stamps were printed by the firm of Rawdon, Wright, Hatch and Edson in 1847. This company and others, some of which had also printed U.S. stamps, merged in 1858 into the American Bank Note Co., which absorbed two other stamp printers, the Continental Bank Note Co. and the National Bank Note Co., in 1879. In 1894 the federal government established the Bureau of Engraving and Printing in Washington, which, with an occasional exception, has since printed all U.S. stamps, bank notes, and other securities.

Canada's first stamps (1851) were also produced by Rawdon, Wright, Hatch and Edson. Later stamps were printed by a Canadian branch of the American Bank Note Co., now the Canadian Bank Note Co. The latter, the British-American Bank Note Co., and Ashton-Potter, Ltd., now produce Canada's stamps.

Great Britain has the largest national industry devoted to the printing of postage stamps.

Perkins, Bacon Ltd., which as Perkins, Bacon and Petch printed the first British stamps in 1840 and stamps for British colonies for many years, suffered bombing damage in World War II but is now providing stamps for some Commonwealth countries. Other long-established British stamp printers, Thomas De La Rue and Co. Ltd., which has absorbed an early stamp printer, Waterlow and Company, and Bradbury, Wilkinson and Co., Ltd., continue to be active. De La Rue has subsidiaries in Nigeria, Pakistan, and Colombia.

Probably the most prolific of the private stamp printers is Harrison and Sons, High Wycombe, England, which produces stamps for more than one hundred postal administrations all over the world and has a daily production that runs to millions of stamps. Harrison and Sons is the principal contractor for printing British stamps in denominations below two shillings and sixpence—Bradbury, Wilkinson prints the higher denominations—and is the main firm for producing the stamps for the British colonies and the stamp-issuing nations that were once a part of the British Empire. It has also printed stamps for the government of Sweden, which found its own facilities too limited to produce certain varieties. Not only is Harrison and Sons famous for the production of stamps for many countries, it is equally noted for its development of photogravure printing processes. When the U.S. Bureau of Engraving and Printing installed presses for the photogravure printing of postage stamps, it sent a team of printers to Harrison's High Wycombe plant for instruction and guidance.

In addition to the British printers mentioned above, the stamp-printing business in Great Britain has created others: Format International Security Printers Ltd.; Walsall Security Printers Ltd.; McCorquodale and Company Ltd.; John Waddington of Kirkstall Ltd.; Questa Color Security Printers; and Alden and Mowbray Ltd.—the Alden Press. Walsall is noted for its free-form self-adhesive stamps produced for the African nation Sierra Leone and the Pacific island of Tonga. These stick to envelopes, but are not easily removable—even by soaking.

Not quite so prolific as Harrison and Sons is Helio Courvoisier S.A. of La Chaux-de-Fonds in the Jura Mountains of Switzerland. The Courvoisier family, settled in the region since the sixteenth century, were first hatters, then publishers and printers, and finally, with the acquisition in the 1920s of a photogravure press which it calls "Heliogravure," stamp printers. The firm's first stamps—for Switzerland—were issued in 1931. Since then, it has printed not only most Swiss stamps but also the stamps of the principality of Liechtenstein and of about sixty other countries. The Swiss postal administration maintains a recess-printing plant in Berne and produces stamps by this process on occasion.

The most venerable stamp printers are Joh. Enschedé en Zonen, operating from a sprawling complex of buildings at Klokhuisplein in Haarlem, the Netherlands. Formed in 1703 by Izaak Enschedé, it took the name of his son Johannes in 1773. Until 1938 there was a Johannes Enschedé in the firm; number VI was the last. One of the world's great printing establishments, producing stamps and newspapers, it is also (since 1743) a typefoundry. The firm has printed all Netherlands stamps except the first (1852) issue, which was produced by the Royal Mint, Utrecht, from engravings made by Enschedé. It has also printed stamps for other countries, although its production has never equaled that of Harrison in England or Courvoisier in Switzerland. Most of the stamp designs used by the firm originate with Enschedé artists and engravers.

Other commercial stamp printers include Imprimerie Delrieu, Paris; Heraclio Fournier, Spain; Suomen Penkin Setelipaino, Finland; Aspioti-Elka, Greece; Ajans-Turk, Turkey; Printex, Malta; Lewin-Epstein Ltd., Israel.

Printing Methods

ALTHOUGH A FEW STAMPS have been produced in other ways, the principal instrument of stamp production has been and is the printing press. The methods chiefly used are:

1. Intaglio, or *taille-douce,* printing
2. Letterpress, also called relief printing or topographic printing
3. Lithography, or offset printing

In recent years, presses have been developed which use a combination of methods. These giant machines with rotating cylinders that print in numerous colors dwarf the single-color flat-bed presses that produced nineteenth-century stamps.

The first stamps, issued by Britain in 1840, were produced by intaglio, a process of printing from a metal plate in which lines have been incised below the surface. Engraving is done with a hard steel cutting knife called a burin, or graver, with which grooves or holes, sometimes minute, are cut into softened metal. These incisions, akin to an artist's brushstrokes, form the "painting" on the metal, defining tones, dark or light, and the essential shadings. Ink is applied to the engraving, sinking into the incised grooves and holes. The surface is then wiped off, leaving ink in the recesses. The paper, on being pressed to the engraving, is driven into the recesses, and the result is an engraved stamp, easily distinguishable by running one's finger lightly over its face.

The plates for the 1840 stamps contained 240 impressions each of the original die, each impression identical to its neighbors except for flaws that crept in during the transfer process or during the punching in of initial letters in the corners of each engraving. The transfer of the original engraved die to the larger printing plate was by mechanical means. The die was hardened and curved over a small cylinder. It was then pressed to the still-soft metal of the printing plate, and, by means of a rocking motion and pressure, the design was impressed in equally spaced areas, one at a time, twelve across and twenty down, on the face of the plate. The completed plate was then hardened, mounted on a base, and printed on a flat-bed press on precut sheets of paper which were then gummed by workmen using brushes. The 1840 stamps were cut apart by scissors, a sharp knife, or a straight-edged device. Stamps did not begin to be perforated until about 1854. Many stamps are still produced by this method and despite numerous technical advances, the craftsman hand-engraver is very much in evidence. While much printing is still from sheet-fed presses, millions of stamps roll from rotary presses using rolls of paper.

Another method of intaglio printing is the gravure process. In gravure printing ink is also drawn up from below the surface of the printing plate. The image, however, is photographed onto the plate, and the design is then chemically etched into it, providing tones, light and dark, in the finished product as the grooves do in the engraving process. The stamp design is usually photographed about four times its eventual size, and the negative checked for flaws. The negative then forms the basis for a series of positives of stamp size, reproduced by means of a step-and-repeat camera that creates a layout on a glass plate. This plate of positives is then projected onto a sensitized gelatin-coated tissue as one might print a photograph from a negative. The tissue has already been screened, producing an invisible grid of very fine lines, projected like the positives. The tissue is pressed onto a cylindrical copper plate. When it is stripped away, it leaves a gelatin film of the screen and design. The plate is then etched with chemicals, the fine lines forming the rims of the minute wells of various depths that take the ink. Once inked, the plate is then scraped with a sharp knife, called a "doctor blade," that removes ink from the areas that are not recessed. Paper pressed onto the plate absorbs the ink. Unlike engraved stamps, which have ridges that can be felt, gravure stamps are smooth and have a silken or velvety feel.

In relief printing, or letterpress, the lines to be printed are raised above the surface of the plate. Relief printing has been carried on since the days of Johann Gutenberg. Most newspapers today are printed by this process. If the touch of the printing press has been too strong, relief-printed stamps—especially when new—may have an impression that can be seen or felt on their backs.

Lithographic printing is based on the fact that oil and water do not mix. Aloys Senefelder, an actor who was also a printer and publisher, invented the technique of lithography in 1798. The word *lithography* results from combining the Greek words for "stone" and "writing." In attempting to wash off greasy printer's ink from a slab of limestone with etching acid, Senefelder discovered that the acid burned off portions of the limestone, but not the area covered by the ink. After many experiments, he found that printer's ink, having penetrated the porous limestone, could not be removed by chemicals; it could only be ground down. When the stone was given a nitric-acid bath and coated with gum arabic, the inked portions, which were undisturbed, could produce a print.

The greasy ink drawings on lithographic stones must be made in reverse; when they are printed, they come out right. Crayon drawings made on paper for transference to printing stones need not be made in reverse; they reverse in the transference. Stamp designs can be transferred from original to stone and repeated as often as necessary.

Much of today's lithographic printing is still done from heavy stone slabs, three to four inches thick. Lighter metal plates have also been developed to carry out the same process.

Offset printing is related to lithography. The printing plate, usually zinc or aluminum and chemically sensitized, is used like a lithographic stone except that once the image has been laid on it by photography and etched, it is bent around the press cylinder. In the printing, the inked plate transfers—offsets—the image onto a rubber cylinder which then imprints the paper as it passes through the press.

Multicolored stamps of the nineteenth century were produced by multiple press runs, the paper being put through the press for each color, one sheet at a time. In the 1920s and 1930s experimental work on multicolor presses for stamp production began in the United States, France, and Italy, but was interrupted by World War II. After the war was over, and engineers could get back to their work, high-speed recess-printing methods were developed that produced multicolored stamps with a single run of paper through a press. The machinery and the method are intricate, and the presses are as fine-tuned as a watch for the proper register of colors.

In an ordinary rotary printing press, printing from either rolls or sheets of paper, inking rollers pass over the printing surface, or plate, which in turn rolls onto the paper as it is fed through the press. The multicolor presses utilize a similar method, except that there are multiple inking rollers. Some of these rollers are carved, or "engraved," so that one can pick up and apply, for example, only brown ink, another red, a third green, at desired areas of the printing plate as it revolves, with the result that at the point where the paper is fed to the printing surface, all the inks have been applied. By putting one color ink over the top of another, a third color can be formed.

FREEDOM FROM WANT

3c POSTAGE

U.S. AMERICA

258. Paul Berdanier, André
Durenceau, and Sam Marsh

Changing the Look of U.S. Stamps

JUST BEFORE WORLD WAR II, a group of American artists, calligraphers, and designers began serious efforts to change the designs of the stamps issued by the United States. They included Rockwell Kent, W. A. Dwiggins, Paul Manship, Leon Helguera, Warren Chappell, Sam Marsh, Walter Dorwin Teague, Clarence P. Hornung, Hugo Steiner-Prag, Edward A. Wilson, Sacha Maurer, Gordon Aymar, Robert Fawcett, Gordon Grant, Paul Shively, Alexander Kahn, George Kanelous, Gustav Jensen, Lucien Bernhard, T. M. Cleland, André Duranceau, Stanley Crane, Clayton Knight, and others. This group worked with Paul F. Berdanier, art director of the J. Walter Thompson advertising agency and a stamp collector long interested in stamp design.

In the spring of 1941, a series of designs, some general, some on defense, were submitted to the Post Office Department. "They were filed away," Berdanier said later. "Nothing was heard about them, but that they had been received." In 1942 designs for a stamp honoring the Czech village of Lidice, which had been destroyed by the Germans, were prepared but rejected by the Post Office. The same year, Francis E. Brennan, who had been art director of *Fortune* magazine before the war and was chief of graphics of the Office of War Information, told Berdanier that designs were wanted for stamps to publicize the war effort of the Allied nations and the Four Freedoms message sent by President Roosevelt to Congress in 1941.

Fifteen designs were offered in mid-November. Archibald MacLeish, head of the Office of War Information, took them to the Post Office Department. On the first anniversary of Pearl Harbor, Brennan told Berdanier that "Franklin Roosevelt has okayed two of the designs." These

259. Sacha Maurer

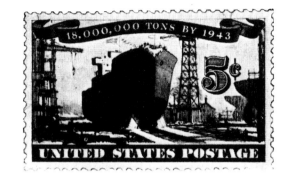

260. Gordon Grant and Sam Marsh

261. Walter Dorwin Teague

262. Gustav Jensen

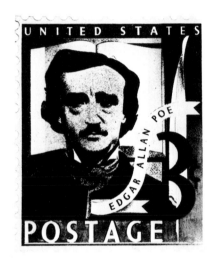

263. Robert Fawcett

264. Paul Berdanier

265. Warren Chappell

266. Clarence P. Hornung

267. Rockwell Kent

268

269

268, 269. Paul Manship's Four Freedoms stamp, 1943, and Leon Helguera's Nations United for Victory stamp, 1943.

270. A stamp in the Overrun Nations series. The series design was produced by the American Bank Note Co. The designer is unknown.

were Paul Manship's design for a one-cent stamp on the Four Freedoms and Leon Helguera's design for a two-cent stamp for Nations United for Victory. The stamps were issued in 1943.

The Berdanier group were elated, and proferred twenty-three designs for stamps in a series to be issued in 1944–45 in honor of the Overrun Nations of Europe. They were not accepted, however. A design from the American Bank Note Company—creator still unknown—was used instead. American Bank Note was given the contract to print the stamps because the Bureau of Engraving and Printing was too busy with other security-printing matters to handle them. The bicolored emission was a drab bit of postal paper in the bank-note syndrome.

Paul Berdanier was killed in a plane crash in August 1945, and his committee's efforts came to a halt. Its goals were not lost, however, for out of it grew the Citizens' Stamp Advisory Committee, formed in 1953 under the aegis of Postmaster General Arthur Summerfield. The members of the committee have changed with changes in administrations, but it has continued to be composed of men and women of similar interests— artists, graphic specialists, historians, and stamp collectors. Similar groups function in other countries, notably England, West Germany, France, and Canada, and the United Nations has its own group.

Since 1953 U.S. stamps have taken on a new look; using new printing techniques and combining classic line engraving with lithography, and, more recently, photogravure, more and more multicolored American stamps have been produced.

Thoughts on Stamp Design

THINGS ON CONSTANT VIEW in everyday life rarely get a second look. With the exception of collectors, artists, and those in the graphic-arts field, most people are rarely aware of that most commonplace of things—the postage stamp. Yet the stamp represents not only payment for the delivery of a letter; it is also a pictograph of the past or present or future and a symbol of the issuing country. The postage stamp as an art form has, the world over, more artists, illustrators, calligraphers, and connoisseurs concerned with it than ever before. Its design is demanding—it must conceive a miniature device to perform a purpose yet also please the eyes of millions of users, many of whom are unaware that it is art.

The illustrations in this book present the creations of hundreds of designers. They are the choice of the author, and there are certain to be differences of opinion as to what stamps should be illustrated. Few of the many stamps that have been issued showing famous paintings or sculpture are illustrated. Too much of the original value is lost in adapting such art to the postage stamp. In the concept of this book, they are not basic stamp designs.

What is good stamp design?

Letters asking this question were sent to a number of well-known stamp designers. They responded with concepts of their own creations or those of other designers:

Stevan Dohanos, Chairman, Citizens' Stamp Advisory Committee, U.S. Postal Service. His paintings and prints are in several art museums, and he is well known for his numerous cover illustrations for the *Satur-*

271

272

273

274

271–80. Sketches by Stevan Dohanos for the United States 1963 Food for Peace stamp, and the finished product (opposite page, below).

day Evening Post and other publications and for his murals in several federal buildings.

The postage stamp . . . carrying an important visual message, has become a significant art form, passing across borders and acting as a nation's calling card. Stamp designing is two-dimensional designing. The artist is given an area, oblong in shape and very small in size, into which he must arrange a great many elements . . . the title and text, the visual symbol or illustrative treatment of the subject matter, the name of the country . . . and the denomination. He is restricted in the number of colors he can use. Historical accuracy is an important consideration.

Proper selection and use of type faces or calligraphy, harmonious with the art, are important considerations in achieving a good design. Some stamps do not require new art because appropriate art or graphics already exist. . . . Paramount must be the relevance and importance of the theme, its visual treatment, its harmony of color, and, above all, the style of its art or graphics. There is nothing more individual than art. It is created by an individual, but judged by many. Stamp art is a graphic statement.

116

275

276

277

278

279

In 1963 Dohanos designed the Food for Peace stamp, one of fifteen that he has created for the U.S. Postal Service. It is his favorite design because of its simplicity and the brevity of its message. He comments:

The stamp . . . addresses itself to the serious problem of malnutrition facing millions of people throughout the world. This design was intended to communicate man's concern for his less fortunate brothers everywhere by illustrating three dramatic and meaningful words: "Food For Peace."

From this concept, a chain reaction of ideas emerged as visual symbols in my mind . . . furrowed land, the plow, a sheaf of wheat, bread, the dove of peace, ways of shipping food cartons to distant places. After many rough sketches, the design idea narrowed to a simple spike of bearded wheat.

The finished art effectively illustrates the message it intended to communicate. It appears in three colors—golden yellow, earth-green background, red in the slogan "Freedom from Hunger." Important to the design is the legibility of the stamp's denomination and the name of the issuing country.

280

117

281. David Gentleman's triptych of
the Prince of Wales Investiture stamps.
Issued by Great Britain, 1969.

David Gentleman, designer of numerous British stamps, illustrator and designer of books, author and illustrator of a series of children's books:

Good stamp design, like good design at any scale, calls for clarity and economy of expression, inherent interest of subject matter and treatment, simplicity and exclusion of inessentials, though this should not, of course, mean boring aridity, careful and sympathetic incorporation of denominations, titles, and so on, as parts of a unified whole.

That much is self-evident. In addition, good stamp design calls for a more indefinable quality of concentration or crystallization of an idea so that it is true-to-scale and not simply a small-scale reduction of a bigger design or picture. In addition, understanding of the printer's problems and capabilities means that the designer can play a great part in insuring that the stamp as printed is as perfect and imaginative as the printing techniques allow; a really good design should be capable of being perfectly printed with only predictable losses (and gains) in production; only an ill-thought-out design can be ruined by the printers.

I think that the triptych of Prince of Wales Investiture designs shows the effects of close cooperation with the printer (Harrison and Sons, High Wycombe) in developing the techniques of several closely allied gray printings in the buildings against the formal metallic background of silver. The use of several grays also enabled me to make sure that window details were individually clear-cut and sharp, which would have been impossible in photogravure if all the gray shades had to be obtained from one printing.

Ole Hamann, chief, United Nations Postal Administration, who has designed more than two dozen stamps for the United Nations:

What is a good stamp design? A difficult question to answer, considering the many different tastes and backgrounds that determine what one considers to be a good design. Basically, I should say that a good design is one in which the composition is simple and clear, the colors in harmony, and the message straightforward and easy to understand.

From the point of view of the United Nations stamps, one can discuss the clarity of the messages conveyed from a good design. This is due to the fact that our subjects are often abstract, such as Economic Progress, Human Rights, etc.

I can point out such a stamp, the thirty-cent definitive, To Unite Our Strength, issued in 1961 and designed by Herbert Sanborn. . . . This design, showing a forward thrust of many different flags, is modern and straightforward. It is obviously appealing to many people, for we have reprinted this stamp a number of times . . . one can almost say on popular demand. Another stamp is the thirteen-cent air mail, 1963,

282. Herbert Sanborn

283. Kurt Plowitz

282–87. Outstanding designs for United Nations stamps, selected by Ole Hamann, chief, U.N. Postal Administration: Herbert Sanborn's 1961 flags stamp; Kurt Plowitz's 1963 13c airmail stamp. *overleaf* Asher Kalderon's 1972 21c airmail stamp; Arne Johnson's 1972 11c birds-in-flight airmail stamp; and two designs by George Hamori, the 1972 World Health Day stamp (adapted from a Leonardo da Vinci drawing) and the Stop Drug Abuse stamp.

284. Asher Kalderon

285. Arne Johnson

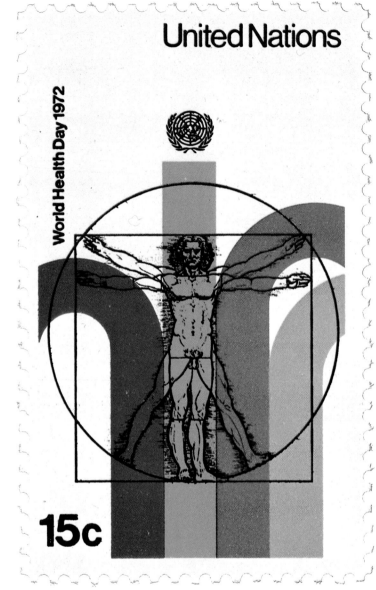

286. George Hamori

designed by Kurt Plowitz, which has the aspects both of air mail and the international character of a U.N. stamp.

There is Olav Mathiesen's eight-cent definitive, 1971, of the U.N. headquarters, A. Kalderon's twenty-one-cent air mail, and the eleven-cent air mail by Arne Johnson, both issued in 1972.

I have stayed away from commemoratives, as the message is quite often more difficult to convey, but I would like to mention George Hamori's World Health Day stamp, 1972, chosen as the second-best stamp design in the world at the Italian Stamp Festival. Then there are Kurt Plowitz's three train stamps for UNICEF, 1966, Eliminate Racial Discrimination, 1971, by D. Gonzaque, and George Hamori's Stop Drug Abuse, 1973.

287. George Hamori

288. Peter Wildbur's 1964 stamp for Ireland commemorating the 200th anniversary of the birth (actually in 1763) of Theobald Wolfe Tone, an eighteenth-century Irish patriot.

Louis le Brocquy, Irish artist now living in France, who has shown paintings in European and American shows and has designed stamps for the Republic of Ireland:

> It is difficult if not impossible, and probably unwise, to attempt to give any verbal definition of a good design in stamps, as with any other designed object.
>
> I have always found it surprising that the first and second stamps ever issued, Britain's Penny Black and Two Pence Blue, 1840, hit the right normal shape and size to which all stamps have subsequently tended to revert.
>
> It is doubtful if their design has been in any important way surpassed. In my view, the most successful design in any Irish stamp was the Wolfe Tone issue by Peter Wildbur, the English typographic designer.
>
> I myself have designed only three stamps and feel that the one which was not accepted was, curiously enough, the best. That was the Irish Civil War commemorative stamp (fifty years) in 1972.
>
> I also designed the Europa stamp for 1970, which was adopted (and adapted) by nineteen other nations, members of the CEPT. The twenty-four strands interwoven represent the member states involved.

The CEPT, Conférence Européenne des Postes des Administrations et Télécommunications, is an organization which annually holds a competi-

122

289. Louis le Brocquy's 1972 stamp for Ireland honoring World Health Day.

290. Louis le Brocquy's Europa stamp for 1970, a flaming sun in the form of a woven fabric. The twenty-four interlaced strands represent the members of CEPT, twenty-four in 1970. See other Europa designs, pages 102–3.

291. Louis le Brocquy's favorite design, proposed for the 1972 commemoration of the Irish Civil War (1922–23), but never issued.

293

294

292–94. Designs honoring Marilyn Monroe, John F. Kennedy, and Sophia Loren, proposed by Czeslaw Slania for United States stamps.

292

tion for a design that can be adapted by member nations wishing to issue stamps commemorating its concept of cooperation.

Czeslaw Slania, who has designed and engraved many stamps—for Sweden, Denmark, Greenland, and his native Poland:

> A stamp is a confirmation of payment . . . similar to currency . . . and is a very important public relations tool . . . distributed in millions of copies. . . . Its graphic level as well as the reproduction testifies in some way about the art of its country. . . .
>
> My best stamps, in my own opinion, were a series for San Marino that were not used.
>
> My favorite motifs . . . are historical paintings by old masters and involve complicated problems of engraving as well as composition. There is a major trend now toward printing such stamps by rotogravure, offset photo-engraving. In my opinion, such stamps have no value. If they are to be printed, it must be by steel engraving.
>
> It is an artistic challenge, and some stamps are masterpieces in themselves. An example is the 1965 U.S. five-cent stamp of Winston Churchill, which is, in my opinion, the best stamp portrait since World War II. Unfortunately, it is anonymous.

295

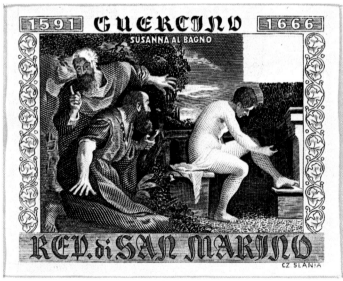

296

295–97. Projected designs for San Marino stamps by Czeslaw Slania.

297

CHURCHILL

U.S. 5 CENTS

298. The United States Winston Churchill stamp, 1965, designed by Richard Hurd from a Yousuf Karsh photograph.

The Churchill design was by Richard Hurd from a Yousuf Karsh photograph. Sam Marsh provided the calligraphy, the engraving of the portrait was by Charles A. Brooks, and the lettering was done by Harold F. Sharpless.

Hatim Elmekki, designer of many stamps of Tunisia:

> In many ways, it is harder to draw a stamp than to paint a masterpiece; a stamp must please everyone, not just the chosen few. The greatness of Rembrandt, da Vinci, Picasso . . . goes beyond the common man's understanding. The artist's work is not conceived for him, even if he is at times overwhelmed by it.
>
> It is just the contrary in the case of a stamp. At everyone's service, it must please all. There is no halfway house. The stamp must make its message clear, usually with a smile. At times, it can even teach, but on one condition: it must not bore.
>
> A good stamp should, in sum, reflect its age. Alas, in these days of constant revolution in art, stamp design remains virtually unchanged. There is one last hope: something new and bright—in the message, the composition, the colors, typography, symbology, and so forth. Sometimes I suffer the constraints of conventional subjects: how can one, for example, design an elating stamp showing the president inaugurating an exposition of chrysanthemums?

300

301

299–301. Tunisian stamps of 1971 designed by Hatim Elmekki: *left,* for a Pan-African telecommunications conference, the Elmekki signature on the tab at top. *center,* a stamp depicting the fifth-century king Bahram-Gur, issued in commemoration of the 2500th anniversary of the founding of the Persian Empire. *right,* a postal recognition of Tunisia's dye industry.

George Hamori, designer of stamps for Australia, Israel, the United Nations, and Papua New Guinea, and creator of industrial designs for Qantas Airways:

> A postage stamp is an important face for a country as it must typify its cities and its industries, its people and their way of life. Stamps . . . mirror the whole country, its respective attitudes, cultures, heritage, and way of life.
>
> Stamps must carry a clear message in an artistic way that will be easily understood. They should appeal to everyone because they can be one of the best propaganda materials of all.

Luis Filipe de Abreu, painter, teacher, graphic designer and illustrator, and designer of Portuguese postage stamps:

> A stamp is something other than a painting, a poster, an advertisement, or an illustration.

302

302–4. Stamps designed by George Hamori: Australia's 1969 commemoration of the fiftieth anniversary of the International Labour Organisation, a 1963 airmail stamp for the United Nations, and a 1968 Papua New Guinea stamp for Universal Suffrage.

303

304

305

306

307

308

305–8. Portuguese stamps by Luis Filipe de Abreu: two for a 1971 Protect Nature series and two for the 1972 Olympic Games in Munich.

What it is exactly is difficult to say. First of all, it is a receipt for a service we pay for, and this is important. . . . There are problems communicating an idea, a concept, sometimes complex and difficult to explain and present in a few inches of picture. Clear interpretation of an idea, easy reading images, small dimensions, but not miniatures, good taste, but not facility, are all important. If there are any obstacles, we try to remove them before reproduction.

For the 1972 Olympic Games series for Portugal, I tried to give a synthesis of movement: a runner almost in starting position, a second "rolling" past, and a third fighting inertia in the final effort. The girls swimming in "dolphin" style are "stroboscopic" images in harmonious undulating movement. These are not naturalistic representations, but synthetic images with which I tried to give a real sensation of motion and time.

THEODORE E. STEINWAY
FÜRSTENTUM LIECHTENSTEIN
1883 1.30 1957
A. PILCH   A. NEFE

309

309, 310. Liechtenstein has honored a number of pioneers of philately, including the Austrian Philippe la Rénotière de Ferrari in 1968 (right) and the American Theodore E. Steinway on a 1972 issue. See also page 43.

Collectors, Stamps, and Philately

WHILE MOST STAMP COLLECTORS refer to themselves by that simple name, certain knowledgeable collectors are called "philatelists," from "philately," a term coined by a French collector, M. G. Herpin, from the Greek words *philo*, meaning lover, and *ateleia*, meaning free of payment. It refers to the intelligent study of postage stamps and their production. Although rather contrived, it is at least an easier term to use than "timbrophilist," which was created from the French word for postage stamp, *timbre*.

Stamp collectors come in all shapes and sizes, all ages, male and female—the whole spectrum of people. King George V of Great Britain, King Carol of Rumania, and King Fuad of Egypt were scholarly stamp collectors. President Franklin D. Roosevelt was a noted collector. Men of position in many walks of life have created outstanding collections; many have made distinguished contributions to research in the field.

Among famous stamp collectors first place goes to Philippe la Rénotière de Ferrari, who was born in 1848 and died in 1917. He began to collect as a child and in his life created a collection of rarities that was probably the most important ever assembled. Ferrari died in Switzerland during World War I; his collection, however, was in Paris, where he had passed much of his life. Since he was an Austrian national, the collection was seized by the government of France as enemy property. After the war, as part of the reparations program it was dispersed in more than two dozen sales, realizing in all about $2 million. Ferrari owned the famous British Guiana One Cent Magenta, which was sold to Arthur Hind, a Troy, New York, plush manufacturer, for $35,000. Hind outbid King

FÜRSTENTUM LIECHTENSTEIN

PHILIPPE DE FERRARI

30

1848

1917

A. PILCH

A. NEFE

310

George V for the stamp, which is the only British Commonwealth stamp not in the Royal Philatelic Collection, founded by the king.

Famous stamp collectors in the U.S. have included Theodore E. Steinway, of the piano-manufacturing family, who specialized in numerous fields, notably in stamps relating to music and musicians; Alfred Lichtenstein, former head of CIBA Pharmaceuticals, and his daughter, Louise Boyd Dale; and the banker Alfred Caspary. The sale of the Caspary collection occupied sixteen auctions in 1956–58 and realized more than $2,800,000. Josiah K. Lilly of the Indianapolis pharmaceutical family; Saul Newbury, a Chicago merchant; John V. P. Heinmuller, president of Longine-Wittnauer Watch Co., who created a fabulous collection of airmail stamps and memorabilia, were all well-known collectors, as was Francis Cardinal Spellman, whose collection is now on display at a museum bearing his name at Regis College in Weston, Massachusetts.

In Europe, Maurice Burrus, an Alsatian tobacco tycoon, almost matched Ferrari in creating a distinguished collection. Theodore Champion of France was made an officer of the Legion of Honor for his contributions to philately and founded a distinguished firm of stamp dealers and philatelic publishers. Carl Lindenberg of Germany and Emilio Diena of Italy were other important collectors.

All these men and women, and many others, built up large and prestigious collections costing a great deal of money, but the membership of the hobby also includes millions of more modest collectors around the world. There are youngsters who find the penny bargain boxes at dealers' shops fabulous mines and those who have the means to acquire items running into four figures.

At the top of the market are items like the unique Mauritius cover with two 1847 penny stamps on it. The stamps were made by the local jewelry engraver so that the governor's wife would have stamps with which to mail out invitations to a ball. At its last sale, the cover realized $380,000.

One can collect topically—for example, stamps showing birds, trees, flowers, or maps. And one collector reportedly formed an interesting collection of stamps that were all purple in color.

Stamps have been collected from about the time of their first emission in 1840. The earliest recorded album for keeping stamps was issued in Paris in 1862 in French, German, and English editions. Immediately after, albums were published in Great Britain and the United States. These albums, as now, had assigned spaces for stamps. In the early days, stamps were pasted in, numerous stamps that would now be rare and valuable being destroyed in the process. Now stamp hinges are used. Hinges are

311. At H. R. Harmer, Inc.'s, auction of the Louise Boyd Dale philatelic estate in 1968, Raymond and Roger Weill of New Orleans paid $380,000—the highest price ever paid for a single philatelic item—for this cover, dated 1850, bearing a pair of the first stamps of the British crown colony of Mauritius. The 1p orange stamps, among the rarest in the world, were created (along with 2p blue stamps of a similar design) by J. Barnard, a Port Louis jewelry engraver, for Lady Gomm, wife of the governor, for use on invitations to a ball. The design of the stamps was adapted from the 1840 Great Britain Penny Black; in error, "Post Office" instead of "Postpaid" was engraved on the left side of the stamp. The cover was inherited by Mrs. Dale from her father, Alfred F. Lichtenstein.

bits of mucilage-coated glassine paper, usually less than half an inch wide and about an inch in length, that are folded over so that about a quarter of an inch of the glue side can be attached to the stamp, the remainder sticking to the album page.

There are many research tools for those collectors who want to know more about their stamps. Many stamp collectors' journals are issued. The Collectors Club in New York, the Royal Philatelic Society in London, and the American Philatelic Research Library at State College, Pennsylvania, all have distinguished libraries.

A COLLECTION OF

RARE AND BEAUTIFUL STAMPS

The Animal Kingdom

312. Grand Cayman terrapin, from the Cayman Islands. 1971.

313. A cockerel was used as the emblem for the Second International Festival of Folk Song. Brazil, 1967.

314. A dolphin (*Tursiops truncatus*), from Senegal. 1970.

137

NOUVELLE-CALEDONIE ET DEPENDANCES

RF

POSTE AERIENNE

PHEULPIN

CONUS LIENARDI

39F

315

315–16. Sea shells of New Caledonia (*Conus lienardi*, 1968, and *Murex brunneus*, 1969).

Horny Coral 3c

Gorgonian

Tokelau Islands

317. Horny coral, from the Tokelau Islands. 1973.

NOUVELLE-CALEDONIE ET DEPENDANCES

RF

100F

MUREX NOIR
(MUREX BRUNNEUS LINK)

PHEULPIN

POSTE AERIENNE

316

318

319

CHERAX COMMUNIS HOLTHUIS 322

PANULIRUS VERSICOLOR (LATR) 323

320

321

324

318–21. Spiny shrimp, fiddler crab, nudibranch, and shell (*Conus clytospira*) from a marine-life series, Mauritius. 1969.

322–24. Lobsters (*Cherax communis* and *Panulirus versicolor*) from a Netherlands New Guinea social welfare fund series of 1962, and a spiny lobster, from Mauritius, 1969.

325. Flying fish decorate an airmail stamp from Western Samoa. 1965.

326. A Blue Marlin, from Mauritius. 1969.

327. Hammerhead sharks (*Zigaena malleus*), from Panama. 1965.

329

330. A praying mantis, from Malawi. 1970.

328, 329. Butterflies: *Danaus chrysippus*, from the Republic of Togo (1970), and *Cyrestis camillus sublineatus*, from Malawi (1966).

331. A wasp (*Polistes gallicus*), from a 1971 Belgian series on insects. The surtax was for philanthropic purposes.

334

335

334, 335. The German Democratic Republic issued a series to publicize the East Berlin Zoo on the occasion of its tenth anniversary, in 1965; an iguana and a group of flamingos are from the series.

332. A rock python (*Python sebae*), from the People's Republic of the Congo. 1971.

333. A tree toad (*Hyla arborea*) from a Polish series on reptiles and amphibians. 1963.

336. Pteranodon, a prehistoric flying reptile, from San Marino. 1965.

337. A tropic bird, from Western Samoa. 1965.

338. A Canada goose, from a "Canada's Resources" series of 1952.

339. A peacock, from Ceylon (now Sri Lanka). 1966.

340. Little gull (*Larus minutus*), from Poland. 1964.

341. A rooster, from a 1971 Iranian series.

342. Lammergeier, from Lesotho. 1971.

343. Crowned cranes, from Ghana. 1959.

344. A boar's tusk (formerly used as currency) and a bird of paradise, from Papua. 1932.

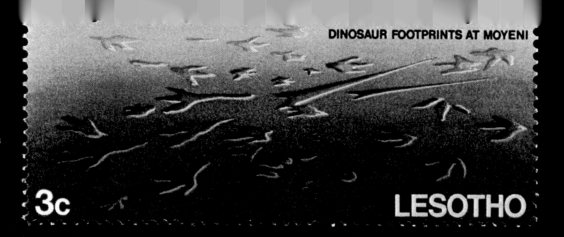

DINOSAUR FOOTPRINTS AT MOYENI

Dinosaur footprints
the trails left by
r tails at Moyeni,
otho, about 200
ion years ago. From
70 Lesotho series on
istoric reptiles.

3c

LESOTHO

RÉPUBLIQUE DE CÔTE-D'IVOIRE

30F

PROTECTION DE LA FAUNE ET DE LA FLORE

POSTES

346. The Kentrosaurus, from a 1970
People's Republic of the Congo series on
prehistoric animals.

JERSEY WILDLIFE PRESERVATION TRUST

Ursine Colobus Monkey

JERSEY 7½p

J. TOOMBS   COURVOISIER S.A.

350. An antelope in the forest, on an
Ivory Coast stamp calling attention to
the need to protect wildlife. 1968.

351. From Japan, a 1971 issue showing
penguins and a map of Antarctica,
issued in honor of the tenth
anniversary of the Antarctic Treaty,
which reserved the continent for peaceful
purposes.

347. An armadillo (*Dasypus hibridus*),
from a series on Uruguayan fauna. 1970.

348. The tapir, an animal indigenous to
Paraguay, is illustrated on a 1961 stamp
celebrating the 150th anniversary of

349. An Ursine colobus monkey, from the Channel Island of Jersey,
part of a Jersey Wildlife Preservation Trust series. 1971.

352. An African elephant, from Ghana. 1964.

353. A horse, from a sixteenth-century print by the Dutch painter and engraver Hendrik Goltzius. Czechoslovakia. 1969.

354. Four animal families appear on this block of stamps issued by West Berlin to commemorate the 125th anniversary of the West Berlin Zoo, 1969.

355. A cocker spaniel, from Bulgaria. 1970.

Architecture

356. St. Paul's Church, Covent Garden, illustrates a 1973 British issue commemorating the 400th anniversary of the birth of architect and designer Inigo Jones.

357. Fan vaulting in the Henry VII Chapel of Westminster Abbey, on a British stamp of 1966 commemorating the 900th anniversary of the founding of the abbey.

358

359

358, 359. In observance of the 1973 Commonwealth Parliamentary Conference, Britain issued a pair of stamps depicting day and night views of London's Parliament buildings.

360. A staircase in Affligem Abbey, Belgium. 1965.

363. Palazzo Vecchio, once seat of the government of the Republic of Florence and now the town hall, was chosen by the Italian government to appear on an stamp of 1961, celebrating the centenary of Italian unity.

364. St. Luke's bell tower in Jajce, Yugoslavia. This view of the fifteenth-century church, the legendary burial place of St. Luke, is from a series issued in 1906, when Jajce was part of the Austrian province of Bosnia-Herzegovina.

361. The Villa Rotonda in Vicenza, built c. 1550, is represented on an Italian stamp honoring its architect, Andrea Palladio. 1973.

362. The U.S.S.R. observed the ninety-second anniversary of Lenin's birth with a stamp picturing the Lenin Mausoleum in Moscow. 1962.

365. The Tower of Cairo, a 629-foot structure with a rotating restaurant at the top, is pictured on a U.A.R. stamp honoring its inauguration in 1961.

366. From a Czechoslovakian series depicting old house signs and portals, a view of the Blue Lion and Old Town Hall, Brno, Czechoslovakia. 1970.

145

POSTAGE

١ بريد

CLOCK TOWER, DUBAI

UNITED ARAB EMIRATES الإمارات العربية المتحدة

367. The Clock Tower at Dubai, from a United Arab Emirates stamp of 1973.

368. The first open-air school in the Netherlands is shown on a Dutch stamp of 1969.

369. The Centenary Memorial Tower and the badge of Hokkaidō, commemorating the 100th anniversary of Japanese settlement and development of Hokkaidō, the northernmost and least populated of Japan's principal islands. 1968.

370

370–72. Postage stamps have helped to publicize international fund drives to save threatened architectural monuments, among them the ancient Egyptian temples at Abu Simbel and on the Nile island of Philae, which would otherwise have been submerged by the Nile after construction of the Aswan High Dam. A United Arab Republic stamp of 1960, commemorating the placing of the cornerstone of this dam, shows the site and the proposed structure. A Qatar series of 1965 presented various views of the monuments, including the Isis temple and colonnade on the island of Philae, and a temple column.

371

372

Art

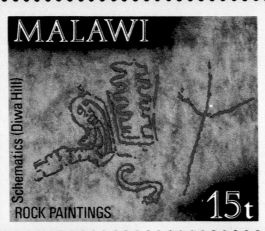

373, 374. Ancient rock paintings from Africa: from Lesotho, *Running Hunters*, from a 1968 series on paintings attributed to the bushmen and their predecessors. From Malawi, figures from Diwa Hill. 1972.

375. A pictograph from Ambrosio Cave, Varadero, Matanzas province, is depicted on a Cuban stamp honoring its Speleological (cave explorers') Society's thirtieth anniversary. 1970.

375

376

377

378

379

380. Marc Chagall, *The Married Couple of the Eiffel Tower*. France, issued 1963.

381. Henri Matisse, *The Blue Nudes*. France, issued 1961.

382. Jean-Auguste-Dominique Ingres, *The Bather*. France, issued 1967.

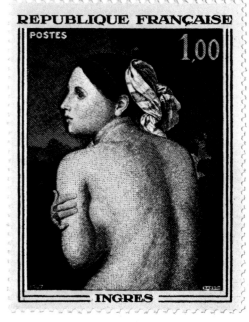

383. Roger de la Fresnaye, *July 14*. France, issued 1961.

148

REPUBLIQUE

FRANÇAISE

DURRENS

AREAREA 1,00

1968 POSTES

P. GAUGUIN

385

386

387

388

389

390

385. To commemorate the centenary of the country's savings and insurance bank, Belgium in 1965 issued this portrait of Peter Paul Rubens by Anthony van Dyck.

386. To commemorate the 500th anniversary of Albrecht Dürer's birth, West Berlin in 1971 issued a stamp reproducing his engraving *The Bagpiper*.

387, 388. Self-portraits: of Heinrich Zille, on a German Democratic Republic issue of 1958 commemorating the centenary of his birth, and a detail from Rembrandt van Rijn's self-portrait of 1639, issued by the Netherlands in 1956 in honor of the 350th anniversary of the artist's birth.

389. *Venetian Woman* by Albrecht Dürer was chosen by Germany for an added-denomination stamp honoring German Art Day and supporting a culture fund. 1939.

390. "Leaving for the Hunt," representing the month of August in *Les Très Riches Heures du Duc de Berry*, a book of illuminated miniatures painted by the Flemish brothers Pol, Herman, and Jehanequin de Limbourg, c. 1415. France, 1965.

391

392

POSTPHILA 1969

393

391, 392. The 500th anniversary of the birth of the painter Lucas Cranach the Elder was celebrated in 1972 by both sections of divided Germany. The German Federal Republic issued a stamp showing a portrait of Cranach from a drawing by Albrecht Dürer; the German Democratic Republic reproduced Cranach's *Resting Spring Nymph* of 1518.

393. *The Painter and the Connoisseur*, a pen drawing of c. 1567 by Pieter Bruegel the Elder, was issued by Belgium as a souvenir sheet to publicize Postphila 1969, an international stamp show held in Brussels. The perforated portion of the sheet, that showing the artist, was for use as a single stamp. Art historians have long debated whether this, too, is a self-portrait.

394. In 1969, in observance of the 450th anniversary of the death of Leonardo da Vinci, Mali reproduced his *Mona Lisa*.

395. *Venus and Amor*, by the sixteenth-century Florentine artist Il Bronzino, was included in an "Old Masters of European Painting" series issued by the Republic of Equatorial Guinea in 1973.

394

395

151

396

396. In 1937, during the Spanish Civil War, German planes sent to aid Franco bombed and destroyed the Basque mining town of Guernica. Pablo Picasso's painting *Guernica*, a memorial to the several thousand slain, now hangs in The Museum of Modern Art in New York. In 1966, Czechoslovakia commemorated the thirtieth anniversary of the establishment of the International Brigades, which fought for the Spanish Republican government against Franco, by issuing a stamp reproducing *Guernica*. Engraver Josef Hercik worked for six months to reproduce this complex painting. The tab, bearing Picasso's signature, shows a detail from the painting —a hand holding a broken sword.

397

397. Picasso's daughter Maia, from a portrait done by Picasso in 1938, when she was six years old, appears on a United Nations stamp issued in 1971 for the U.N.'s International School.

400

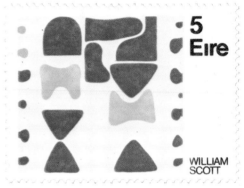

398

399

398. Eugène Delacroix's *Moroccan Saddling Horse* (1855), from a series reproducing paintings at the Hermitage museum in Leningrad. U.S.S.R., 1972.

399, 400. *Berlin Blues I* by William Scott, one of a series of contemporary art stamps from Ireland, 1973, and, from the same series, a detail of *Madonna of Eire* by Mainie Jellett, 1970.

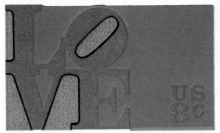

401. Robert Indiana's Pop Art *Love* was used for a U.S. stamp in 1973; the stamp was reissued in 1974.

402. *Winter Day* by Pekka Halonen, issued by Finland in 1965 in honor of the centenary of the artist's birth.

403, 404. Nudes on stamps: from Romania, a study by Nicolae Tonitza, and from Yugoslavia, *Little Gypsy with a Rose*, by Nikola Martinoski. Both were issued in 1969.

401

402

403

404

405–9. From the Netherlands, a series of designs created by computer. These engraved designs are akin to the machine-turned engravings of the first stamps, in the nineteenth century. On these stamps the background tints have been laid down over the entire printed sheet.

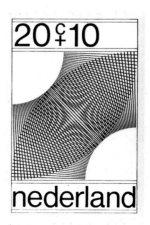

405

406

407

408

409

411. A scene of village life by Goto Narcisse, issued by the Republic of Chad, 1970.

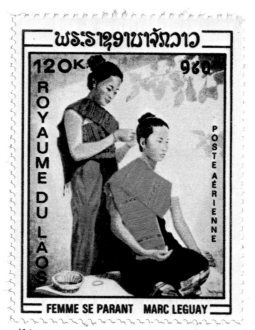

412. *Family Living in a Valley* (sometimes called "Chasing the Cat") by the Korean artist Sodang (Yi Chae-gwan), 1783–1837. Republic of Korea, 1971.

415. *Enchanted Owl*, a print by the Eskimo artist Kenojuak, on a Canadian stamp of 1970 honoring the centenary of the Northwest Territories.

416. From the People's Republic of China, from a stamp series called "The Glorious Mother Country," a representation of *Celestial Flight*, adapted from the T'ang Dynasty murals at Tun-huang, Kansu province. 1952.

417. A partridge and a fig-pecker, part of a fresco at Knossos, Crete, c. 1500 B.C. From a Greek series on Minoan art. 1961.

418. A mural by Mrs. Gabriel Ellison in Mulungushi Hall, Lusaka, was reproduced by Zambia on a stamp commemorating the Non-Aligned Nations Summit Conference in 1970.

410. A detail from a painting by Kano Naganobu, *Dancer from Flower Viewing Party*. Japan, 1962.

413, 414. Kokei Kobayashi, *Sisters Combing Hair*, issued by Japan in honor of Philatelic Week, 1969. From Laos, *Laotian Women* by Marc Leguay, a French artist who lived in Laos after 1936. 1969.

154

413

414

REPUBLIQUE DU DAHOMEY

POUR VENISE UNESCO

POSTE AERIENNE

35 F

BASIL. S. MARC, VENISE - PAVEMENT A MOSAIQUE (XII SIECLE)

DELRIEU

419

420

421

419–21. Numerous stamps have urged the rescue of Venice from the waters eroding its buildings. In 1972 Dahomey pictured a section of mosaic from St. Mark's Basilica, showing a stork devouring a snail; Tunisia depicted the prow of a gondola; and Cambodia (the Khmer Republic) presented a stylized design showing the Lion of St. Mark.

422. A detail of a sixteenth-century Slovak St. Michael icon depicts the archangel expelling Adam and Eve from the Garden of Eden. Czechoslovakia, 1970.

423. A fresco from the fifteenth-century monastery church of Voronets, in the Moldavian region of Romania. 1970.

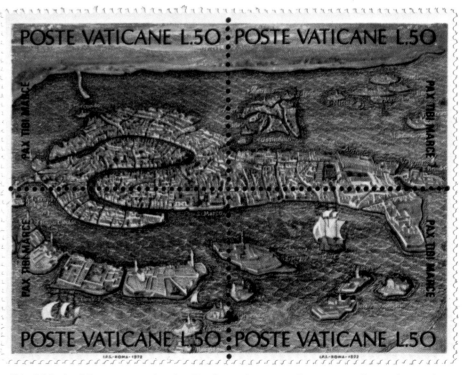

424. A block of four stamps showing Venice as it appeared on a map of 1581, from a fresco in the Gallery of Maps, the Vatican, painted under the direction of Ignazio Danti. Vatican City, 1972.

425

426

425, 426. Portions of two French cathedral windows: The Madonna and Child from the rose window of the Cathedral of Notre-Dame, Paris; and St. Paul on the Road to Damascus, from the Cathedral of St.-Etienne at Sens. Both stamps were issued to commemorate the 800th anniversary of the cathedrals—Notre Dame in 1964 and St.-Etienne in 1965.

427. This 1973 issue is one of a series of six Israeli stamps depicting Marc Chagall's stained-glass windows for the Hadassah-Hebrew University Medical Center Synagogue in Ein Karem, Jerusalem.

428, 429. The 12-by-15-foot Marc Chagall stained-glass window in the lobby of the United Nations Secretariat Building is reproduced on a U.N. souvenir sheet of 1967. The entire sheet was slit-perforated so that the six portions, of varying sizes, could be used as individual postage stamps—"United Nations" and the denomination (6c) appear at various points along the borders of the sheet. In addition, a portion of the design, from the top center of the window, was used for a single stamp entitled *The Kiss of Peace.* 1967.

427

428

UNITED NATIONS • 6c   UNITED NATIONS • 6c   UNITED NATIONS • 6c

CHAGALL
WINDOW
1967

UNITED NATIONS • 6c   UNITED NATIONS • 6c   UNITED NATIONS • 6c • MARC CHAGALL

429

BARRA MEXICANA 1922 1972
JUSTINIANO
CORREOS MEXICO
H. RODRIGUEZ T.I.E.V. 1972
40 ¢

430. A Mexican mosaic depicting the Byzantine Emperor Justinian I, who codified Roman law, is reproduced on a Mexican stamp of 1972 commemorating the fiftieth anniversary of the Mexican Bar Association.

ARRASY WAWELSKIE

POLSKA 1 15 zł

DETAIL FROM THIRD CENTURY MOSAIC
UNITED NATIONS 6¢

DÉTAILS D'UNE MOSAÏQUE DU IIIᵉ SIÈCLE
NATIONS UNIES 13¢

431

432

431, 432. An ostrich and a pheasant, details from a third-century mosaic found at Haidra, Tunisia. The complete mosaic, *The Four Seasons and the Genius of the Year*, is at the United Nations, a gift from Tunisia. The United Nations issued these stamps in 1969 as part of a series on art at the U.N.

433. Iran in 1970 honored the International Congress of Architects in Isfahan with a stamp depicting an ancient Persian tile.

434. In 1970 Poland issued stamps depicting details from a collection of 136 tapestries made in Brussels in the sixteenth century, and now in Wawel Castle Museum, Krakow. This stork is from the series.

6R. IRAN
ISFAHAN INTERNATIONAL CON-

433

434

435

436

437

438

439

440

441

442

443

444

445

435. A design of sculptured figures commemorates the twenty-fifth anniversary of the National Federation of Austrian Social Insurance Institutes. 1973.

436. A relief from an eleventh-century rune stone on the island of Öland, Sweden. 1961.

437. The twelfth-century Black Virgin from Montserrat, a Benedictine abbey, from a Spanish issue of 1956.

438, 439. Sculptured cupids from the Fountain of Diana, Versailles. France, 1952.

440. The sixteenth-century *Nuremberg Madonna*, by Paul Vischer, on a German Federal Republic stamp of 1952 celebrating the centenary of the founding of the Germanic National Museum at Nuremberg.

441. French stamp of 1930 showing the head of an angel from the west portal of Reims Cathedral. Her smile has such appeal that it has become known in popular tradition as the "Sourire de Reims."

442. Olympic rings and a horseman from a carved slab at Clonmacnoise, Ireland, appear on a stamp issued by the country in 1972 to honor the Twentieth Olympic Games in Munich, and the fiftieth anniversary of the founding of the Olympic Council of Ireland.

443. A gargoyle from the Bern Cathedral, issued by Switzerland in 1973.

444. Prince Albert I of Monaco was a distinguished oceanographer and student of paleontology. This portrait statue by François Cogne is in the Gardens of St. Martin, Monaco. 1951.

445. Czeslaw Kaczmarczak and Stefan Malecki joined talents to create this double memorial issued by Poland in 1965 to commemorate the city's 700th anniversary. The background of the souvenir sheet is the ancient seal of Warsaw. The stamp in the lower right-hand corner reproduces a memorial statue to those who died in defense of the city in World War II.

446. Appealing for international assistance for victims of a 1970 earthquake, Peru depicted this petroglyph from the area devastated by the quake. 1970.

447. From Poland, a ceramic ram of about 4,000 B.C., uncovered by archaeologists. 1966.

448. The six-armed Asura from the Kōfuku-ji, Nara, Japan. From a series on art treasures of the Nara period. 1968.

446

447

448

449

449. A Polynesian stone deity, from the Pitcairn Islands. 1971.

450. A head carved of pierre de M'Bigou, a type of stone named after a town in southern Gabon. Gabon, 1973.

451. An Ife bronze head, from the Yoruba country of western Nigeria, tentatively dated A.D. 1000–1400. From a Nigerian pictorial series, 1953–57.

452. From Cyprus, a stone head of the third century B.C. 1971.

453. From a San Marino series on Etruscan art, a duck-shaped pitcher of the third or fourth century B.C. 1971.

454. A detail from the Lions' Gate of Jerusalem's Old City wall. Lions flank a tablet commemorating Suleiman the Magnificent, who rebuilt the city walls in the sixteenth century. An Israeli issue of 1968 honoring Tabira, the National Philatelic Stamp Exhibition in Jerusalem.

450

451

452

454

455

455. Wood carvings from Nigeria, honoring the second anniversary of the proclamation of the Republic of Nigeria, 1965.

456

458

459

456, 457. Two issues from Papua and New Guinea depicting tribal art: a carved canoe prow from the Sepik district (1965), and a *malanggan* carving from the island of New Ireland (1963).

458. A carved screen from Uganda, commemorating the Thirteenth Commonwealth Parliamentary Conference, held there in 1967.

459. A carved cross and other religious figures from Dahomey, celebrating the World Festival of Negro Arts in 1966.

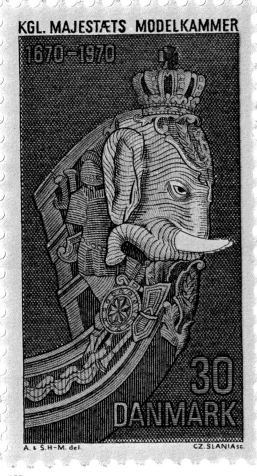

460

460. Denmark commemorated the 300th anniversary of its Royal Naval Museum in 1970 with a stamp picturing a ship's figurehead of an elephant, made about 1741.

461. A Swedish souvenir sheet of 1969 reproduces wood sculptures salvaged in 1961 from the Swedish ship *Wasa*, which sank in Stockholm harbor while leaving on its maiden voyage on August 10, 1628.

461

Aviation and Space

462. The first officially issued postage stamp in the world to depict an airplane was this United States parcel-post issue of 1912.

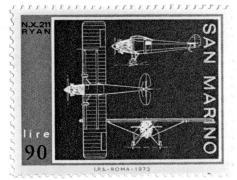

463. Charles A. Lindbergh's *Spirit of St. Louis*, from a San Marino series on famous airplanes. 1973.

467–70. Three stamps of 1969 from Great Britain honoring the Anglo-French Concorde, the supersonic airliner, and a 1968 issue from the New Hebrides showing the plane.

467

464. A Zoegling training glider, from Switzerland. 1946.

468

465. To commemorate one of the first international flights between Greece, Rhodes, Italy, and Turkey, Greece in 1926 issued this stamp showing an Italian Savoia S–55 twin-hulled flying boat superimposed on a map of the eastern Mediterranean.

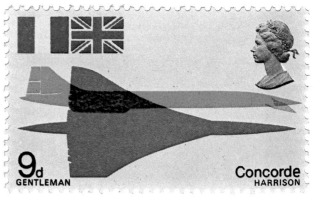

469

466. The first Hungarian aircraft is pictured on this 1959 stamp, one of a series issued to publicize the country's Museum of Transportation.

470

RETROSPECTIVE
DE L'ESPACE

POSTE AERIENNE

ICARE

25F

REPUBLIQUE GABONAISE

luna69

aéreo $2 méxico

473

1969 ČLOVĚK NA MĚSÍCI

60h

ČESKOSLOVENSKO

474

2.50 POLSKA

475

1 РУБЛЬ · ПОЧТА 1961

СССР

СЛАВА КПСС!

СЛАВА СОВЕТСКОМУ НАРОДУ!

476

15¢

mala

seteshen sate

477

c15 SEMANA DE
AERONAUTICA 1947

CORREOS

REPUBLICA ARGENTINA

471, 472. In a 1970 series on forerunners of space flight,
Gabon pictured the legendary Greek character Icarus, who
flew too close to the sun; the heat caused the wax joints of
his wings to melt, and he fell into the sea and perished.
In observance of Aviation Week in 1947, Argentina, too,
pictured Icarus's fall.

СССР
ПОЧТА 1971

«ЛУНОХОД-1»

K16

473. Mexico recorded
first footstep on the mo
1969, on a stamp issued
(See also pages 66–69.)

474. Czechoslovakia h
man on the moon, and
of Manhattan Island. 1

475. Poland commemor
Russian group space fl

476. From the U.S.S.R.
of space flight, engrave
aluminum-surfaced pap

477. Malaysia, in a ser
the earth satellite stat:
depicted an antenna fo
signals. 1970.

478. The U.S.S.R. inve
to explore the surface
one of these, the Luna
depicted on a stamp fr

Business and Industry

479

480

481

482

479. For the 1964 United Nations Conference on Trade and Development, held in Geneva, a U.N. stamp designed by Herbert M. Sanborn.

480–82. Banking, as represented on a Philippine stamp honoring the seventieth anniversary, in 1971, of the First National City Bank in Manila; a 1971 issue celebrating the opening of a new branch of the Bank Negara Malaysia, since 1967 the sole currency-issuing power in Malaysia; and a Greek issue of 1966 commemorating the 125th anniversary of the founding of the National Bank of Greece.

483. Old Manilla (bracelet) currency, from a Nigerian series issued 1953–57.

484. A suggestion of stock-market graphs, to commemorate the centenary of the Sydney Stock Exchange. Australia, 1971.

485–87. The old and new Irish currency as reflected on Irish stamps: a dog on an ancient brooch from Killamery, county Kilkenny; and a winged ox, symbol of St. Luke the Evangelist, after the Gospel Book of Lichfield Cathedral, from a series issued 1968–69; values are expressed in shillings and pence. The new decimal currency, with values expressed by numerals only, is represented by a 1971 stamp showing a stylized elk.

483

484

485

486

487

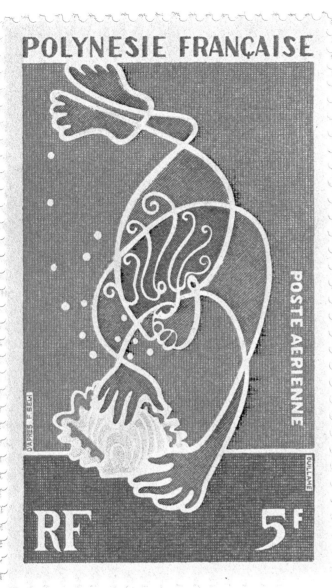

490. Plastics used in buttons and in building, from Finland. 1971.

491. A refrigeration slaughterhouse, from Chad. 1969.

492. Austria celebrated the centenary of the Vorarlberg embroidery industry in 1968.

493. An illustration from a sixteenth-century book was used on a Spanish stamp marking the Fourteenth World Tailoring Congress, held in Madrid. 1970.

494. From Qatar, divers at work on an undersea oil pipeline. 1972.

488. A pearl diver, from French Polynesia. 1970.

489. Making paper umbrellas, Thailand. 1973.

1c BOATBUILDING ANGUILLA

495. Boatbuilding, from the independent Caribbean island of Anguilla. 1970.

6 PESOS

EL CHOCON - CERROS COLORADOS

REPUBLICA ARGENTINA

CASA DE MONEDA   "XII—1969"   E. MILIAVACA Dib.

496

496, 497. Argentina depicted the El Chocon-Cerros Colorados Electric Power Project as part of a national development series of 1969; South Africa pictured the Hendrik Verwoerd Dam, the main reservoir of the Orange River Project, on a 1972 stamp issued to mark the dam's inauguration.

RSA

10c

H F Verwoerddam 1972   Clive Lindsay

497

1½d

GHANA TIMBER

GHANA

498

500. Fiji included forestry development in its national development series of 1973.

5c Fiji

FORESTRY DEVELOPMENT

500

498, 499. Logging, as represented by Ghana (1959) and the New Hebrides (1969). Around the New Hebrides stamp are border designs showing aspects of the local timber industry.

E II R   R F

INDUSTRIE DU BOIS

KADRI

POSTES   20 CENTIMES OR

CONDOMINIUM DES NOUVELLES HÉBRIDES

499

25 R·P SHQIPERISE

25 TETOR 1970

ELEKTRIFIKIMI I GJITHE FSHATRAVE TE VENDIT

1944   60 67   1970

501

501. Albania in this 1970 issue celebrated the twenty-fifth anniversary of the completion of rural electrification.

502. Kenya, Uganda, and Tanzania jointly celebrated the fifth anniversary of the African Development Bank, in 1969, with a design showing the bank emblem and a euphorbia tree in the form of a map of Africa.

BANQUE AFRICAINE DE DEVELOPPEMENT
AFRICAN DEVELOPMENT BANK

Fifth Anniversary   1964-1969

AFRICAN DEVELOPMENT BANK

KENYA UGANDA TANZANIA   1'50

502

Census

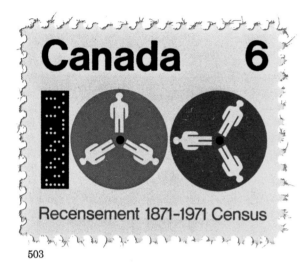

503

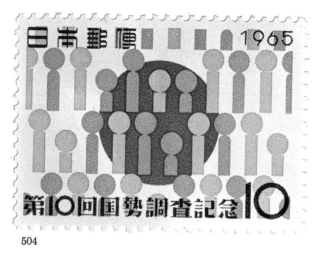

504

505

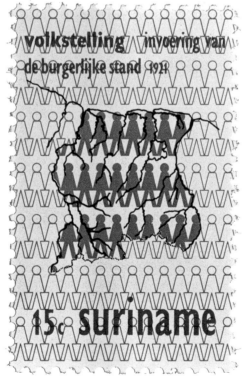

507

508

506

503–11. Census-takers have been busy around the globe. Canada celebrated the centenary of its national census in 1971 with a stamp depicting cutout figures superimposed on computer-tape reels; Japan pictured Kokeshi dolls and the Japanese flag in commemorating its tenth national census, in 1965. Luxembourg and Poland used similar figures for their national-census postal stamps, both issued in 1970, as did Surinam, commemorating the fiftieth anniversary of its census, in 1971. Norway issued a pair of stamps representing punch cards and stylized figures to commemorate the 200th anniversary of its national census in 1969. The Ryukyu Islands showed stylized faces on a stamp noting its 1970 census. Venezuela, for its 1971 national census, presented a crowd scene, in the shape of a question mark.

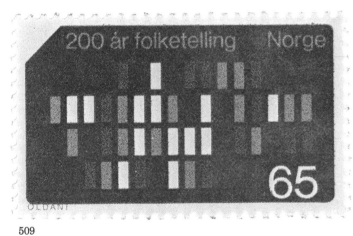

509

510

511

Communication

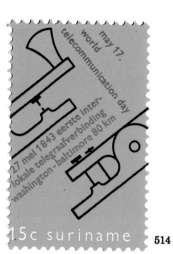

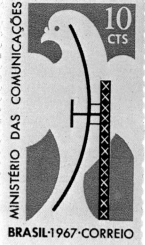

514

515

512. Italy commemorated the completion of its trunk telephone dialing system with a design of a telephone dial and wires. 1970.

513. The German Federal Republic saluted its television industry with a representation of a light effect on a television screen. 1957.

514. For World Telecommunication Day, 1971, Surinam recalled the first telegraph, between Washington, D.C., and Baltimore in 1843, with this design of a Morse-code key.

515. Brazil depicted a radar beam projected on the outline of a pigeon, an early means of delivering messages. 1967.

516. On the centenary of the founding of the newspaper *La Nación*, Argentina honored its founder, Bartolomé Mitre. 1969.

517. The Strijdom Tower, an FM radio tower in Hillbrow, Johannesburg, named in honor of Johannes Strijdom, former prime minister of South Africa, is pictured on a 1971 stamp commemorating the tower's inauguration.

518. Celebrating the centenary of its submarine cable to England, in 1970, Portugal issued a stamp depicting a cable ship.

519, 520. Cuba honored the twelfth congress of the International Association of Publishers in 1971; San Marino depicted rotary-press rollers in commemorating a Tourist Press Congress in 1973.

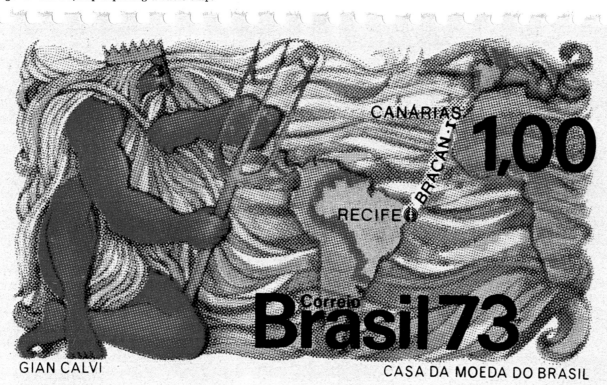

521. Commemorating the completion of an underwater telephone cable between South America and the Canary Islands, Brazil in 1973 depicted a rough map of the south Atlantic and the sea god, Neptune, with his trident.

Conservation

522. A United Nations issue of 1960 honored the Fifth World Forestry Conference in Seattle, Washington.

523. A 1972 issue from the Netherlands showing the area involved in its historic Delta Plan, which called for filling in the delta area, shortening the coastline by more than 400 miles, and providing a supply of fresh water.

524. Cyprus called attention to European Nature Conservation Year, in 1970, with a series of landscapes.

MONACO

0,50

POLLUTION DES EAUX DE MER

F. BEL - G. VIENNE - JACANA - SC. JUMELET

525

RSA 3ᶜ WATER 70

526

525, 526. Monaco showed a dying sea bird in a 1971 issue campaigning against pollution of the seas and South Africa called attention to the need for preservation of fresh water in 1970.

Crafts and Other Techniques

527–29. From French Polynesia, a series on the native arts of the Marquesas Islands: mother-of-pearl carving, carving of ornamental earrings, and tattoo design. 1967–68.

530, 531. Embroidery from Cyprus, 1971, and eighteenth-century embroidery from Ioannina, Epirus, Greece, 1966.

532. An Algerian rug, from Kalaa. 1968.

533. Folk-art paper cutouts, from Poland. 1971.

534. A woodcarver from Syria and a sample of his work, issued in honor of the Seventeenth Damascus International Fair in 1970.

535. Woven baskets from the Pitcairn Islands, from a series celebrating native handicrafts. 1968.

177

REPUBLIQUE FEDERALE DU CAMEROUN · POSTES FEDERAL REPUBLIC OF CAMEROON

5 F

ABBIA - SYMBOLE DE LA REPRODUCTION

536

60c

PAPUA & NEW GUINEA

537

PARIWISATA 1973

BALI

100₸

REPUBLIK INDONESIA

538

REPÚBLICA PORTUGUESA

CORREIOS

5 Cents.

Arte Indígena

TIMOR

CASA DA MOEDA

539

536. Fertility symbol from Abbia, Federal Republic of Cameroon, 1969.

537. A headdress from the Chimbu district of Papua and New Guinea. 1968.

538. From Indonesia, a ceremonial mask from the island of Bali. 1973.

539. Silver hollow ware, from the Portuguese overseas territory of Timor. From a series on indigenous art, 1961.

540. An eighteenth-century pistol, from Algeria. 1970.

541. A twelfth-century Polish coronation sword. 1973.

542. From a 1970 Hungarian series on masterpieces from the country's National Museum, in Budapest, and Treasury, in Esztergom, a silver and gold tankard made in 1690.

543. Luxembourg in 1967 issued a series of stamps commemorating the 200th year of the manufacture of Luxembourg faience. This shaving dish of 1819 shows a wedding scene by the artist Charles Degrotte. 1967.

544. A drinking horn, made in the second century B.C., from the Turkmen Republic, a constituent republic of the U.S.S.R. From a U.S.S.R. series on the State Museum of Oriental Art. 1969.

PISTOLET. XVIIIᵉ siècle

1,00

ALGERIE

TEMAM.

540

SZCZERBIEC · XII W.

50 GR POLSKA

541

FEDELES DISZKUPA · 1690.

3 Ft

MAGYAR POSTA

1970.   LEGRADY S.

542

200 ANS FAIENCE LUXEMBOURGEOISE

LUXEMBOURG 1.50F

COURVOISIER S.A.

543

ПОЧТА CCCP

ГОСУДАРСТВЕННЫЙ МУЗЕЙ ИСКУССТВА НАРОДОВ ВОСТОКА

РИТОН · ТУРКМЕНИЯ · II ВЕК ДО Н.Э.

4 КОП.   1969

544

Education

545

546

547

545–49. Educators and scholars: In 1969 the Netherlands celebrated the 500th anniversary of the Dutch scholar Desiderius Erasmus of Rotterdam, and in 1944 Ireland marked the 300th anniversary of the death of Michael O'Clery, a Franciscan lay brother. O'Clery was one of four historians who compiled *Annals of Four Masters*, a history of Ireland from earliest times to the beginning of the seventeenth century. In 1970 Italy commemorated the centenary of the birth of Maria Montessori, and in 1946 Switzerland commemorated the 200th anniversary of the birth of Johann Heinrich Pestalozzi; both were reformers who have had great influence on primary education. The German Democratic Republic in 1958 honored the seventeenth-century Czech educator and theologian J. A. Komensky (Comenius), who developed the first textbook with pictures adapted for teaching children; the stamp, depicting Comenius teaching, is based on an old engraving.

548

549

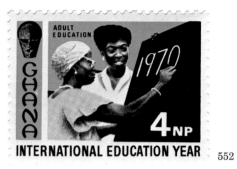

550 551 552

550–52. Many nations honored International Education year in 1970 with stamps of similar design, among them Ethiopia and Cuba. A stylized abacus appears on the Cuban stamp. Ghana's postal tribute to International Education Year stressed adult education, showing a woman at a blackboard learning to write.

554

553. In 1969, for the Week of the Blind, Morocco issued a stamp depicting hands reading Braille.

555

554–55. A pupil practices the alphabet on a Haitian stamp of 1969; Qatar displays a child reading, commemorating the tenth anniversary of Education Day in Qatar (1971).

556. The outline of a mortarboard is superimposed on a map of the South Pacific area on this Fiji issue of 1969, marking the inauguration of the University of the South Pacific at Suva.

Entertainment

557

558

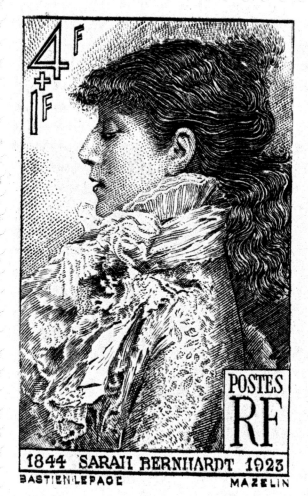

559

557–58. Two 1966 issues from Greece celebrate the heritage of Greek drama: one depicts a copper tragic mask from the fourth century B.C., the other, the ancient theater of Dionysus in Athens. Both stamps are part of a series commemorating the 2,500th anniversary of the inauguration of the First Contests of Drama by Pisistratus, Tyrant of Athens, in 534 B.C.

559. A portrait of Sarah Bernhardt by Jules Bastien-Lepage was adapted for this French stamp of 1945, commemorating the centenary of her birth and honoring the Coquelin Foundation, a home for aged actors.

560. To commemorate the fiftieth anniversary, in 1970, of the Habimah National Theater, Israel issued this stamp showing a scene from the company's production of An-Ski's tale of possession, *The Dibbuk*.

561. Laotian stamp of 1969 depicting a scene from the Indian epic *The Ramayana*, performed by the Ballet Royal of Laos.

560

181

562. A film strip issued by West Berlin for the Twentieth International Film Festival, held there in 1970.

566. The puppet Pulcinella, from a West Berlin added-denomination Welfare Fund series of 1970.

565. Auguste and Louis Lumière, inventors of the cinematograph, and portraits of Jean Harlow and Marilyn Monroe are shown on this Mali issue of 1970.

563. In 1971 the People's Republic of the Congo issued a series of stamps on "cinema personalities," including this one of Marilyn Monroe.

567. From the German Democratic Republic, a Sorbian dance costume. 1971.

564. Walt Disney's cartoon character Donald Duck appears on a stamp issued by the Republic of San Marino in 1970.

568. The magician Robert Houdin and his floating-boy trick are shown on a French issue of 1971. The latter-day magician Ehrich Weiss adapted the name, calling himself Harry Houdini.

569. Austria pictured a ferris wheel from the Prater Amusement Park, Vienna, on a 1966 issue celebrating the 200th anniversary of the park.

570. Carole Joan Crawford, Miss Jamaica of 1963, was crowned Miss World the same year. She is shown on a Jamaican stamp issued on Valentine's Day, 1964.

571. A performer on a unicycle juggling hoops. Romania, 1969.

572. Gilbert and Ellice Islands youth in costume for the Ruoia dance. 1965.

573. A South Pacific dancer's mask from the Leipzig Ethnological Museum is illustrated on a German Democratic Republic issue of 1971.

574

574, 575. Native dancers depicted on stamps from Swaziland (1968) and Zambia (1964).

Exploration

576, 577. In 1972 Western Samoa commemorated the 250th anniversary of the discovery of Samoa by the Dutch admiral Jacob Roggeveen with two stamps. The one pictured above shows a map of Roggeveen's Pacific voyage, during which he also discovered Easter Island; the other shows Roggeveen's three ships being tossed about on a stormy sea.

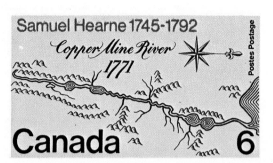

578. In 1956 New Hebrides observed a double anniversary—the fiftieth anniversary of the Condominium (a form of joint British-French administration) and the 350th anniversary of the discovery of the islands in 1606 by the Portuguese navigator Pedro Ferñandez de Quirós.

579. A Bulgarian issue of 1973 depicts underwater photography being used in the exploration of the Black Sea.

580. Canada's Copper Mine River and Arctic coast were discovered by Samuel Hearne of the Hudson's Bay Company in 1771. A map of the area appears on a Canadian stamp of 1971 honoring Hearne.

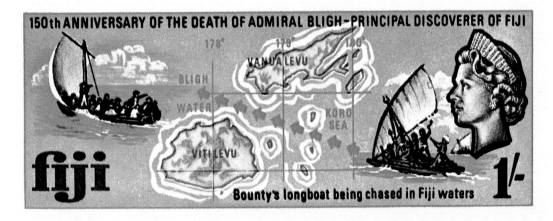

581. In 1967 Fiji commemorated the 150th anniversary of the death of Admiral William Bligh, who explored the archipelago during his 4,000-mile journey in the longboat of the H.M.S. *Bounty*, into which he had been cast adrift by a mutinous crew. The stamp shows Bligh and his men being chased from Fiji waters.

582. The ascent of Mount Gasherbrum II, 26,363 feet high, in the Karakorum Mountains in Kashmir, by an Austrian team on July 7, 1956, is commemorated on an Austrian stamp of 1957, on the first anniversary of the Himalaya-Karakorum Expedition.

583

584

583, 584. The first settlement of a new territory has often been an occasion remembered with a stamp issue. The British colony of Seychelles commemorated the 200th anniversary of the first settlement on Saint Anne Island in 1970 with an image of an abandoned ship's anchor. Brazil, celebrating the 400th anniversary of the founding of Niteroi, in 1973, depicted one of its original aborigine inhabitants, a costumed warrior.

585. Henry Morton Stanley was sent on his first expedition to Africa to look for the ailing explorer Dr. David Livingstone and, when they met, is supposed to have greeted him with a casual "Dr. Livingstone, I presume." From a 1973 Republic of Burundi series commemorating the Livingstone-Stanley explorations.

Expositions

587   588   589   590

586. In 1958 the United States presented an aerial view of its pavilion, designed by architect Edward Durell Stone, for the Brussels World's Fair of that year.

591

587–91. For its role at EXPO '67 in Montreal, Canada, the United Nations issued five stamps, sold only at and valid for use only from the U.N.'s Montreal pavilion. Four designs by Ole Hamann, representing Peace, Justice, Fraternity, and Truth, were based on a bas-relief by Ernest Cormier for the U.N. entrance doors, donated to the organization by Canada in 1951. The fifth stamp, designed by Olav S. Mathiesen after a photograph by Michael Drummond, was a colorful presentation of the U.N. pavilion.

592

593

592, 593. A New Zealand stamp publicizing EXPO '70, held in Tokyo, presents the EXPO '70 emblem and an abstract drawing of the New Zealand pavilion's Geyser Restaurant. Australia also represented its EXPO '70 pavilion on a stamp issued that year.

594. The United States went all out for EXPO '74 in Seattle, plugging EXPO's theme, "Preserve the Environment," with a colorful Peter Max poster.

Government and Politics

A párizsi kommün 100. évfordulója

3 Ft

MAGYAR POSTA

NAGY Z.

596

100 ЛЕТИЕ ПАРИЖСКОЙ КОММУНЫ

VIVE LA COMMUNE

КОП 6

ПОЧТА СССР 1971

597

100 JAHRE PARISER KOMMUNE

20 DDR

Barrikade auf der Place Blanche, die von Frauen verteidigt wurde

595

595–98. Although France did not commemorate the centennial of the Paris Commune in 1971 with stamps, the anniversary was recognized by a number of other countries. The German Democratic Republic showed the barricade at Place Blanche; Hungary pictured a detail from François Rude's sculpture *La Marseillaise*, from the Arc de Triomphe; the U.S.S.R. depicted fighters at the barricades; and Yugoslavia adapted its commemoration from A. Lamy's *Proclamation of the Commune, March 28, 1871*.

1,25

1871–1971

JUGOSLAVIJA

598

REPUBLIQUE FRANCAISE · POSTES

0,65

PRISE DE LA BASTILLE 14 JUILLET 1789

599. A French stamp of 1971 recalls the storming of the Bastille on July 14, 1789.

600, 601. Two West Berlin issues: for the tenth anniversary, in 1959, of the ending of the Berlin blockade, a design showing U.S. Air Force planes, and a 1956 stamp showing the *Luftbrücke* (aerial bridge), the airlift memorial erected in Berlin.

602. Germany in 1944 commemorated the twenty-first anniversary of the Beer-hall Putsch, Hitler's abortive attempt to overthrow the state government of Bavaria, in Munich, with this stamp showing the German eagle killing the serpent of Communism.

603, 604. For the twentieth anniversary of the International Federation of Resistance Fighters, in 1971, the German Democratic Republic reproduced these lithographs from Fritz Cremer's *Buchenwaldzyklus*.

605, 606. In 1965 Great Britain celebrated the 700th anniversary of its Parliament. Two British issues of that year show the seal of Simon de Montfort, earl of Leicester, who in 1265 called together the first Parliament, and a view of Parliament House (now St. Stephen's Hall), Westminster Hall, and the east end of Westminster Abbey after a seventeenth-century engraving by Wenceslaus Hollar.

607. Canada honored the 200th anniversary, in 1958, of the meeting of the first Canadian Parliament with a stamp showing the mace and speaker's chair.

608. A Polish issue of 1969 marking the Fifth Congress of the United Peasant Party.

609, 610. A Japanese issue of 1960, honoring the Forty-ninth Inter-Parliamentary Union conference, shows the seating plan of the Japanese Diet. A Mexican stamp of similar design commemorated the twenty-fifth anniversary of the United Nations General Assembly in 1970.

611. Libya's position in the Middle East conflict is reflected in this 1971 commemorative to Al Fateh, the Palestinian guerrilla movement.

612. Kuwait in 1971 called attention to Palestine International Week with a design showing Palestine superimposed on a globe.

613. A Pakistani stamp of 1970 commemorating the country's first general election, held that year for both provincial and national assemblies.

614, 615. A 1968 issue from Iran calls attention to the Twelve Royal Reforms instituted by Shah Mohammed Reza Pahlevi; the block of stamps composing a fanwheel, issued in 1969, reflects the continuation of these reforms.

616. A calligraphic remembrance from the Netherlands marking the centenary, in 1972, of the death of the Dutch statesman Johan Rudolph Thorbecke, quoting in Dutch his statement "There is more to be done in the world than ever before."

613

614

616

615

617. Malta honored the Migrants' Convention, held there in 1969, with a stamp (below) showing swallows in flight—symbolic of sons and daughters returning to the native hearth.

618. This 1972 stamp from Iceland, depicting the continental shelf, was issued to call attention to the country's offshore fishing rights. The shelf provides breeding grounds for fish, which account for 80 percent of Iceland's exports.

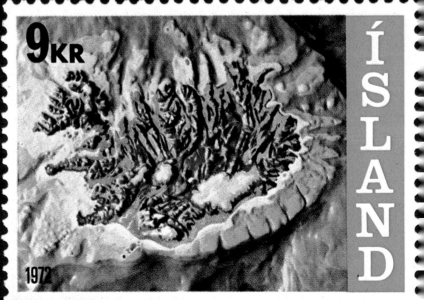

TALLERES DE IMP. DE EST. Y VALORES-MEXICO

619

620

619, 620. To commemorate the inauguration of President Manuel Avila Camacho in 1940, a Mexican stamp issued that year shows a ship's helmsman, symbolic of the executive. The Philippines in 1973 issued a commemorative honoring Carlos P. Garcia, fourth president of the country.

621–23. In 1967 Southwest Africa, a mandated territory administered by the Republic of South Africa, released these memorials to Dr. Hendrik F. Verwoerd, prime minister of South Africa who was assassinated in 1966. The camel-thorn-tree design bears the English slogan "Steadfastly Strong;" that of the sea pounding the rocks, "Firm as a Rock." The other languages are Dutch and Afrikaans.

621

622

623

624. The fiftieth anniversary of Interpol, the international police force, was commemorated by a 1973 stamp from the German Federal Republic symbolizing the organization's international radio communication.

625. Hungary noted the 1973 Conference on European Security and Cooperation, held in Helsinki in 1973, with an image of Europe held in two cupped hands.

626. The fiftieth anniversary of the consolidation of the boroughs into the City of New York, in 1948, is commemorated in this United States stamp designed by Victor S. McCloskey, Jr.

627. Uruguay in 1972 paid its respects to Dan A. Mitrione of the Agency for International Development. Mitrione, an American advisor to the Montevideo police, was murdered by Tupamaro terrorists in 1970.

Historic Documents

The reproduction of historic documents on postage stamps necessarily entails extreme reduction in size, even taking into account the large stamps currently being issued. Normally the words on these documents cannot be read on the stamp without the use of a strong magnifying glass.

628. In 1598, in an attempt to resolve religious conflicts in France, Henry IV promulgated the Edict of Nantes, defining the rights of the country's Protestants. France, 1969.

629. The text of a Fidel Castro declaration is spread across five Cuban stamps. 1964.

630

630, 631. *Enosis* (union) with Greece, which has long been demanded by some Greek Cypriots rebelling against British rule of the island, has been fiercely resisted by Turkish Cypriots. In 1954 the British Parliament offered Cyprus limited self-government but rejected *enosis*, refusing to consider any change in British sovereignty over the island. In protest, Greece issued stamps that reproduced the text of the British Parliamentary debate in Greek, English, and French—the English and French on stamps used for overseas airmail—and implanted what it called "a blot of shame" on the text to register its anger.

LONDON · PARLIAMENTARY DEBATES · HOUSE OF COMMONS
Official report · Wednesday, 28th July, 1954 · Cyprus

Mrs. LENA JEGER (Holborn and St. Pancras, South):... For many years we have not taken the question of ENOSIS sufficiently seriously. I should like to remind the House of the words of the right hon. Gentleman the Member for Woodford (Sir WINSTON CHURCHILL), who visited Cyprus when he was Under-Secretary at the Colonial Office. He said to the Legislative Council in Cyprus: «I think it is only natural that the Cypriot people who are of Greek descent should regard their incorporation with what may be called their mother country as an ideal to be earnestly, devoutly and fervently cherished. Such a feeling is an example of the patriotic devotion which so nobly characterizes the Greek nation.»— Mr. R.H.S. CROSSMAN (Coventry, East): When was that said?— Mrs. JEGER: That was said to the Legislative Council in 1907. I think that the right hon. Gentleman's words are eternally true...— Mr. E. L. MALLALIEU (Brigg): We should have offered before now a proper solution which, if the Government had not had its head in the sand, would have been the one most likely to further not only the interest of the Cypriots but our own.— Mr. R.HS. CROSSMAN (Coventry, East): I wonder why the hon. Gentleman and some of his friends opposite object so much to certain actions of Soviet Russia? To what do they object? Here is the principle that where military security is concerned we have the right to occupy a country, whatever its national ownership may be, to disregard all plebiscites or elections, and to tell those people that it is good for them to be under our rule. I wonder whom we think we are deceiving? Whom do we think we are taking in with all these ridiculous announcements and this talk from the other side? I wonder who will be deceived by the Minister's statement about all the good we have done for Cyprus, and how we really want to give them self-government — but, of course, not to let them do what they want to do. Oh, no — we give them everything else and deny them what they really want. This has been going on for a long time. We have been told by those opposite that this island had never been under Greek sovereignty. It happens to be the only one of the hundreds of islands of Greece which is not part of Greece proper. It is not part of Greece proper because Disraeli swopped it with the Turks in 1878. It became part of Britain in 1878, and believed that as a Colony of Britain it would get independence, but it is as a result of being a British Colony that it has been denied the independence and ENOSIS which have obtained by every other one of the Greek islands. To the Cypriots we say, «It is all for your good. We know you better than you know yourselves.» There are some 10,000 Cypriots who have come to Britain and have their own ideas about this. But we know better than them. Even when under the great influence of this Metropolis they remain obstinately convinced of their grievance and remain in favour of ENOSIS; they feel Greek; they are Greek — even then hon. Gentlemen say «No, no, gentlemen — with time and trouble we shall teach you not to be Greek.» How often in our colonial history have we said the same thing? It is an ironical fact that we are starting the trouble in Cyprus on the same day as we have the ignominious end of the trouble in Egypt. May I say to hon. and right hon. Gentlemen opposite that this retreat from Egypt is a scuttle. Hon. and right hon. Gentlemen said, «We shall be tough. We shall not give way. Where our national security is concerned we stand ... BEVAN (Ebbw Vale): The speech to which we have just listened is characteristic of the courage and honesty of the hon. and gallant Member for the Isle of Ely (Major LEGGE BOURKE). He is very plain spoken about these matters, and perhaps he was quite right when he said that in one respect this was a black day for Britain... The hon. and gallant Member for the Isle of Ely is quite right when he is so sorrowful about the situation. What he is now saying is that Great Britain has not changed her attitude to the world at all, that we have not adjusted ourselves to the facts of the modern world, and that we are still as imperialist as we ever were but we are not as strong as we were...

631

194

Health and Welfare

632. Malta presented a scene of early medical treatment, and the Congress emblem, on a stamp commemorating the First European Congress of Catholic Doctors, in 1964.

633

634

635

636

637

638

639

640

641

633. Iran honored the fiftieth anniversary of its Midwives' School, in 1970, with an issue depicting a baby-carrying stork.

634. An Ethiopian added-denomination stamp showing the Tree of Health, issued for an anti-tuberculosis fund. 1951.

635. The German Federal Republic pictured nurses in honoring Wilhelm Löhe, founder of an establishment for deaconesses, on the centenary of his death, in 1972.

636. South Africa honored the Forty-seventh Congress of the Medical Association of South Africa, in 1969, with a series of stamps calling attention to Dr. Christian Barnard's pioneer human-heart transplant operation at Grote Schuur Hospital, Capetown, in 1967.

637, 638. In 1921 insulin was discovered by two Canadian doctors, Frederick G. Banting and Charles H. Best. Observing the fiftieth anniversary of the discovery in 1971, Canada depicted the instruments and materials used by the researchers in the laboratory of the University of Toronto Medical School. A Belgian issue of 1971, also observing the anniversary of the discovery, pictured the insulin molecular diagram and test tubes.

639. Stamp from Afghanistan showing the human heart, issued to commemorate World Health Day, 1972.

640. The DNA (deoxyribonucleic acid) molecule and chart appear on a stamp issued by Spain on the occasion of the Sixth European Congress of Biochemistry. 1969.

641. A Tunisian Red Crescent stamp of 1972 portrays an aged man.

642

643

644

645

642, 643. The battle against cancer is depicted on a French stamp by an allegorical figure, representing Science, in combat with a hydra, and on a United Nations stamp by a man wrestling with a giant crab. The French added-denomination stamp, issued in 1941, was for a cancer fund; the United Nations issue honored the Tenth International Cancer Congress of the International Union Against Cancer, held in Houston, Texas, in 1970.

644, 645. Rehabilitation is a key to the return to health. Finland represented the rehabilitation of invalids as a seated man playing volleyball. 1970. Luxembourg, in a series of added-denomination stamps issued to promote a charity fund in 1968, pictured a lovely child, underscoring the cruelty of mental handicaps.

646. France, among other nations, has taken note of the crucial role of blood donors. 1959.

647. Belgium honored the twenty-fifth anniversary of Belgian social security in 1970.

648

649

650

651

648. Belgium showed people adrift in an open boat in this 1927 "Caritas" stamp in the Art Nouveau style, an added-denomination issue for tuberculosis and war victims funds.

649. To help build its Children's Village fund, Costa Rica made the use of its 1967 Madonna-and-Child stamp obligatory on all mail.

650. In 1922 the German Reich issued a 12M. stamp, eight marks of which went for a fund for children and the aged.

651. A Tunisian issue of 1973 stressing family planning.

652, 653. Children's faces were used on an Austrian stamp of 1966, issued to celebrate the tenth anniversary of the Save the Child Society, and on a German Democratic Republic issue of 1971 commemorating the twenty-fifth anniversary of UNICEF.

654. Luis Filipe de Abreu designed the 1973 children's-aid stamp for Portugal.

652

655. Road safety for children is the theme of this 1971 Austrian stamp.

656, 657. Children's drawings appeared on a 1965 Netherlands Child Welfare stamp and a 1970 Yugoslavian stamp commemorating Children's Week.

658. Swiss stamp of 1916 showing a dairy boy from the Bernese highlands, one of a *Pro Juventute* ("For Youth") series. The funds from the sale of these stamps went to youth-aid programs.

659, 660. The United Nations Children's Emergency Fund has been the subject of many stamps issued by the U.N. The 1951 first issue "Helping Hand" was designed by Sem L. Hartz of the Netherlands; the 1961 stamp showing a mother bird feeding her young was designed by Hisano Minoru of Japan for the fifteenth anniversary of UNICEF.

661. A Singapore issue of 1970 marking the tenth anniversary of the Singapore People's Association, which raises funds and provides recreational programs for children.

662. One of a 1970 series of Child Welfare stamps from the Netherlands.

655

658

656

659

661

Holidays, Festivals, and Special Events

663

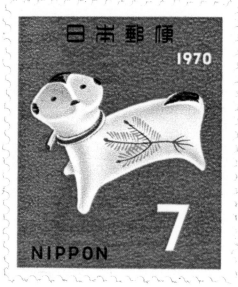

664

665

666

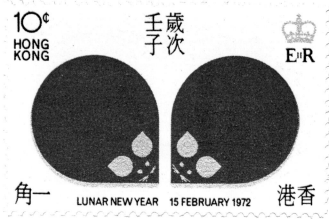

667

663–67. In Asia the New Year is linked by name to an omen animal—for example, the Year of the Rat or the Year of the Boar. (Because the years are determined according to a lunar calendar, the dates do not coincide with Western ones. Most of these stamps were issued in December of the year mentioned; the Hong Kong Lunar New Year stamp was issued in February.) Some samplings from the Orient's New Year's stamps include the straw snake from Japan, 1964; a clay guardian dog of Hokkeji, made for Empress Komyo in the Tempyo Era, 1969; a kite from Korea, and a piggy bank from the Republic of China (Taiwan), both to celebrate the Year of the Boar, 1970; and a 1972 Year of the Rat issue from Hong Kong.

668

699

668. Children's handmade clay toys are shown on this Pakistani issue commemorating Universal Children's Day, 1967.

669. From Syria, a lovely presentation of a boy and girl and a rose, celebrating the Fifth Youth Festival at Homs. 1969.

670. From Laos, a 1957 issue reproducing a Laotian miniature, *The Cutting of the Hair*. This ceremony, which the Laotian boy undergoes at the age of thirteen, marks his transition from childhood to pre-adult life.

671, 672. Christmas night in the Bahamas and the Gilbert and Ellice Islands. 1971.

671

672

673

673, 674. The Virgin and Child theme on stamps from the Gilbert and Ellice Islands, 1969, and Malawi, 1970.

674

680

680, 681. Children have often designed Christmas stamps; not surprisingly, Santa Claus has figured prominently on a number of their creations. Nine-year-old Anthony Martin provided a Canadian design for 1970; Edison Thérésine showed Santa Claus riding a turtle on a 1971 Seychelles issue.

681

682–84. The U.S.S.R., too, observes the Christmas season and the start of the New Year. A dove, symbolizing peace, and a globe appear on a stamp issued in late 1962 for the New Year of 1963. Santa and a *troika* in front of the Spasskaya Gate tower, the Kremlin, are shown on a December 1971 stamp issued for the New Year of 1972; and a Christmas tree and a tower of Spasskaya Gate are featured on a stamp issued in late 1970 for the New Year of 1971.

682

683

684

676–78. Chevalier E. V. Cremona is responsible for most of Malta's stamp designs, including these, issued for Christmas 1967.

679. The United Sta[...] first issued Christma[...] stamps in 1962. Doll[...] Tingle, the wife of American stamp des[...] Ward Brackett, put needlework to good[...] in designing this Christmas issue. 197[...]

675

676

677

678

679

685

686

687

685–87. Jennifer Toombs adapted Albrecht Dürer woodcuts *The Last Supper*, *The Crucifixion*, and *The Resurrection* for a series of Easter stamps issued in Antigua, 1971.

689

688–90. The carnival spirit, as represented on stamps from St. Vincent (1969) and Trinidad and Tobago (1968); and Chanticleer, the Pheasant Queen of Malaya, from Trinidad and Tobago (1970).

690

691. Austria in 1935 commemorated Mother's Day with a stamp reproducing *Mother Love*, a painting by the nineteenth-century artist Joseph Danhauser.

688

693. A tug-of-war performed during the rice harvest celebration on the Ryukyu Islands, from a 1969 festivals series.

694

692. For its Vernal Equinox Festival, Bulgaria in 1973 issued a series of stamps depicting celebrants' masks, from designs by V. Vassileva, including this one from the Hisar region.

694. Dragon mask worn in a Macao processional. 1971.

695. The Pentecost Island land-divers of the New Hebrides perform a ritual whose origin is lost in the islanders' history. Men dive from an eighty-foot tower, with long vines attached to their ankles. The vines are exactly long enough to break their headlong plunge just short of the earth. From a 1969 New Hebrides series on the divers.

695

Human Rights

696. For the nineteenth triennial meeting of the International Council of Women, in Bangkok in 1970, Thailand projected a map of the world against a background of Thai temples, with the council emblem.

697

698

699

700

697–704. After 1971 was declared the International Year for Action to Combat Racism and Racial Discrimination, a number of nations issued stamps emphasizing the theme of racial equality. Shown are 1971 stamps from Brazil, the Cameroons, Guyana, Kuwait, Pakistan, Turkey, Zaire (then the Democratic Republic of the Congo), and the United Nations.

701

702

703

704

206

705

706

707

705–7. Stamps have called the world's attention to the plight of refugees. In 1953 the U.N. issued a stamp calling for protection of refugees; in 1958 the U.N. General Assembly adopted a resolution to promote a World Refugee Year, dating from June 1959, to encourage government and civic agencies and individuals to make contributions to the World Refugee Fund. In 1960 France issued a stamp showing a girl standing amid the ruins of a city to honor World Refugee Year. A Norwegian stamp of 1971 commemorated the Nordic countries' aid to refugees.

708. In 1961 Egypt portrayed a mother and child behind barbed wire to publicize its annual Palestine Day.

Independence

Finland
Independence 1917-67

United States **5**c

POSTA ČESKOSLOVENSKA

709. The short-lived Provisional Government of Russia, which overthrew Czar Nicholas II, prepared this chain-breaking stamp, symbol of freedom from Czarist bondage. In the October Revolution of 1917, the Provisional Government was itself overthrown, and it was the new Soviet government that actually issued this stamp for the Russian Socialist Federal Soviet Republic in 1918.

710. In 1967 the United States joined in observing the fiftieth anniversary of Finland's independence.

711. In 1919, celebrating the first anniversary of its independence, Czechoslovakia presented the Lion of Bohemia breaking its chains.

EIRE **5P**

POSTAGE OF IRELAND

REPUBLIC OF IRELAND

1 ONE CENT **1**

THE
FENIANS
1867~1967

éire

in Ainm
na Críonóide
Ro-Naomda

2P bunreact na héireann 2P

712, 713. An Irish issue of 1937, celebrating Ireland's new constitution, shows a young woman (Eire) with her right hand resting on a harp, having just written the first words of the new constitution. An Irish issue of 1967, commemorating the centenary of the Fenian Rising, a movement which aimed to overthrow British rule, reproduces Fenian labels prepared in the United States at the time of the insurrection for use in independent Ireland. More than likely these were the work of a notorious faker, S. Allen Taylor.

ISRAEL – 25 YEARS OF INDEPENDENCE   ישראל לעצמאות שנים 25

ISRAEL ישראל   1.00

PRICE - IL 1.50   המחיר - ל״י 1.50

714. Among Israel's postal observances of its independence, a souvenir sheet commemorating the country's twenty-fifth anniversary, in 1973, reproduced the Israeli Declaration of Independence. The lower, perforated portion could be removed for use as a single stamp.

715. For the twenty-fifth anniversary of its independence, in 1972, Pakistan issued a series of designs; this one represents land reforms.

716   717   718

  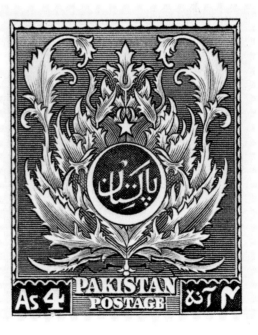

716–18. In 1947 Britain partitioned India to form two independent nations, India and Pakistan. A Pakistani stamp of 1948 celebrating independence depicts a crescent and stars, an Urdu inscription, and a Saracenic leaf pattern. Two 1951 issues, celebrating the fourth anniversary of independence, show a symbolic lamp of learning and a similar Saracenic pattern.

বাংলাদেশ
POSTAGE REVENUE Rs. 2
Bangla Desh

719

১৬ই ডিসেম্বর
বিজয় দিবস
16th December
VICTORY DAY

৬০প বাংলাদেশ 60P
BANGLADESH

720

ALGER 1962
INCENDIE DE LA BIBLIOTHEQUE
0.20 UNIVERSITAIRE +0.05
ALGERIE POSTES

721

20д
1962
FÊTE NATIONALE
RÉPUBLIQUE TUNISIENNE

722

FEDERATION OF NIGERIA

COMMEMORATION OF INDEPENDENCE 1960 1'3d

723

OVERHEAD CABLE CARRYING ASBESTOS
INDEPENDENCE 1968
SWAZILAND 4½c

724

1'30
UHURU 9th. DEC. 1961
TANGANYIKA

REPUBLIC OF BIAFRA
Second Anniversary May 30th 1969
4d

NIGERIA
1970
ONE PEOPLE
ONE DESTINY
1/-

Свободу
народам
Африки!
ПОЧТА
4 коп
1961
CCCP

719–20. Pakistan, as created by the British partition of India in 1947, consisted of two discrete areas, separated by almost 1,000 miles of India. In 1971, East Pakistan revolted and achieved independence as Bangladesh. A 1971 stamp issued by Bangladesh describes the 1970 election results that precipitated the independence struggle: "167 seats out of 169 for Bangladesh—98%." A year later, the young Bengali nation commemorated "Victory Day," December 16, 1971, with a stamp showing a flight of doves. 1972.

721. Algeria in 1965 recalled the burning of the Algiers University Library three years earlier by foes of Algerian independence.

722–25. Independence issues from African nations: from Tunisia, celebrating National Day, 1962; from Nigeria, 1960, depicting a map of Africa, torch, and dove; from Swaziland, a series representing national resources, this one showing an overhead cable carrying asbestos from Havelock Mine to a railway at Barberton; and from Tanganyika (later united with Zanzibar to form the Republic of Tanzania), a freedom torch and Mt. Kilimanjaro.

726, 727. The Republic of Biafra in 1967 declared itself independent from Nigeria, precipitating a bitter three-year civil war, which Biafra lost. For the second anniversary of its Independence Day, in 1969, Biafra depicted a child in chains against a world map. In 1970, Nigeria commemorated the reintegration of Biafra and the establishment of the Federation of Twelve States with this "One People—One Destiny" issue.

728. The Soviet Union joined in celebrating postally the independence of African nations. A 1961 issue commemorating the Third Conference of Independent African States shows a map of Africa and an African breaking a chain.

729. The United Nations commemorated the independence of all nations which gained their independence after 1945 with fireworks. 1967.

729

Literature

730

731

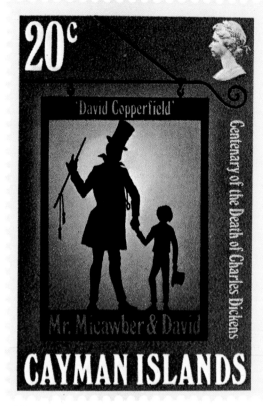

732

733

734

733, 734. Two Turkish issues of 1957, one honoring the 750th anniversary of the birth of the theosophist and poet Mevlâna (Jalal-al-din Rumi) and the other, the 400th anniversary of the death of Fuzuli (Mehmet Suleiman Oglou), a poet admired for his love lyrics.

735. Painter Jack B. Yeats prepared twelve watercolors as illustrations for *The Aran Islands* by J. M. Synge. One of these watercolors, *An Island Man*, was reproduced on an Irish stamp of 1971, marking the centenary of Yeats's—and Synge's—birth.

735

730. Portuguese issue of 1972 marking the 400th anniversary of the publication of Luiz de Camoëns's epic poem, *The Lusiad*, a celebration of the discoveries of Portuguese navigators in the East Indies. Camoëns was shipwrecked off the coast of Cambodia and lost everything but the manuscript of the poem, hence the image on the stamp.

731, 732. For the centenary of the death of Charles Dickens, in 1970, the Commonwealth state of St. Kitts–Nevis–Anguilla portrayed the graveyard scene—Pip meeting the convict—from *Great Expectations*, and the Cayman Islands presented Mr. Micawber and David from *David Copperfield*.

736. In 1970, to honor the author Herman Melville and the whaling industry, the United States issued this embossed envelope by Bradbury Thompson showing Moby Dick.

737. Baron Hieronymous Karl Friedrich von Münchhausen, whose adventures inspired some of the tales in Rudolph Erich Raspe's *Baron Münchausen's Narrative of His Marvellous Travels and Campaigns in Russia*, was remembered by the German Federal Republic in 1970, on the 250th anniversary of his birth.

738, 739. The poet and dramatist William Butler Yeats and the dramatist John Millington Synge were honored by Ireland in 1965 and 1971, on the centenaries of their respective births.

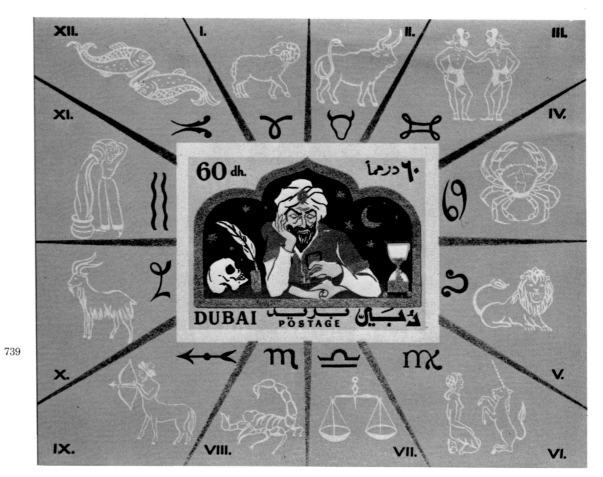

740. Dubai's 1967 tribute to Omar Khayyám, the eleventh-century astronomer-poet of Persia, whose most famous work is the *Rubáiyát*.

213

743. "Puss 'n Boots," from the seventeenth-century children's classic by Charles Perrault, appears on a Republic of Mali issue of 1972.

741, 742. For International Book Year, 1972, the Vatican showed a page from a small codex of St. Paul's Epistle to the Romans found in central Italy in the fourteenth century. Israel honored International Book Year with a design suggesting a turning page.

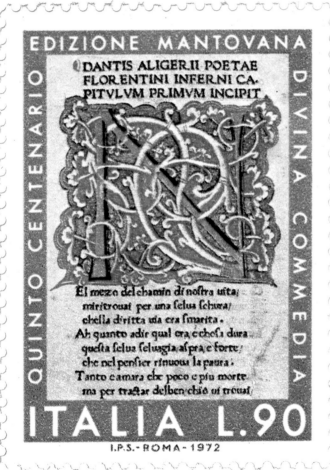

744. A Swedish issue of 1971 illustrates Selma Lagerlöf's classic children's story, *The Wonderful Adventures of Nils*, with a picture of Nils Holgersson riding on the back of a goose.

745. A bookplate of the Vilnius University Library in the U.S.S.R. is shown on this Russian stamp of 1970 commemorating the library's 400th anniversary.

746. For the 500th anniversary of the publication of Dante's *The Divine Comedy*, Italy in 1972 reproduced the initial letter and first verse from the first printed book.

747. In observance of the 500th anniversary of book-printing in Hungary, the country issued this stamp depicting typesetting, from a woodcut reproduced in *Orbis Sensualium Pictus* by the seventeenth-century Czech theologian and educator Comenius. 1973.

748. For the fiftieth anniversary of Interpol, the international police force, in 1972, Nicaragua issued a series on famous detectives, which included this stamp of Arthur Conan Doyle's Sherlock Holmes, as portrayed by the actor Basil Rathbone.

Maps

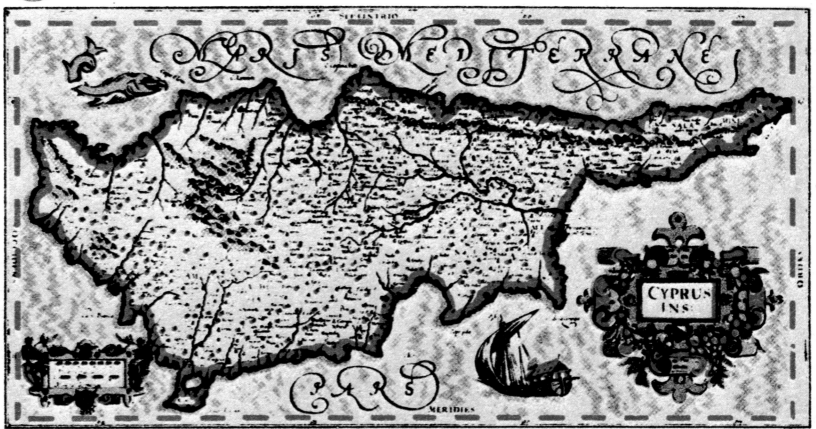

749. For the first International Congress of Cypriot Studies, in 1969, Cyprus issued a stamp showing a medieval map of Cyprus.

750

751

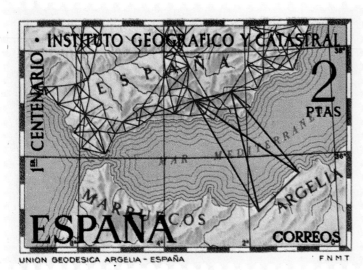

752

753

750. How to represent the earth's curved surface on a flat piece of paper, without distorting the size or shape of any of the continents, has always been a problem for mapmakers. One solution is the sinusoidal projection, in which all parallels of latitude appear as straight lines evenly spaced, while meridians of longitude appear as curved lines. This projection appeared on a U.N. stamp of 1964, designed by Ole Hamann.

751. In honor of a visit by Queen Elizabeth II, Malta depicted the queen with an outline map of the Maltese islands. 1967.

752. A survey map of the western Mediterranean area was used on a Spanish stamp of 1970 commemorating the centenary of the Geographical and Survey Institute.

753. Grenada, southernmost of the Windward Islands, and its dependency island, Carriacou. 1966.

754. Artifacts are superimposed over a map of the island Republic of Nauru. 1973.

755. Look closely at the red background of this Romanian stamp—it is a map of Europe, issued in honor of a conference on Inter-European Cultural and Economic Cooperation. The black lines, which look rather like telephone switchboard lines, are links between European capitals. 1970.

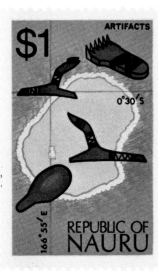

754

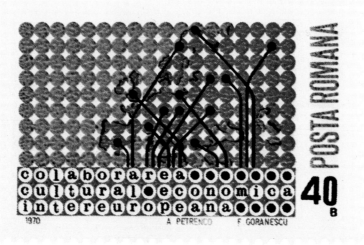

755

Minerals

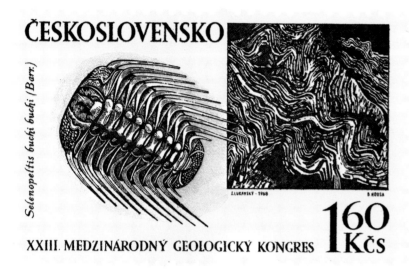

756, 757. Czechoslovakia honored the twenty-third International Geological Congress, in 1968, with a series of stamps depicting various minerals. One shows silurian schist from central Bohemia (approximately 420 million years before present) and a trilobite fossil (approximately 460 million years before present). A German Democratic Republic issue of 1969 shows calcite.

Music

758

761

759

760

762

763

758–60. Symbols of music: a lute, horn, oak branch, and laurel leaves were used in a Bradbury Thompson design for a U.S. stamp commemorating the fiftieth anniversary of the American Society of Composers, Authors and Publishers (ASCAP) in 1964; a winged figure holding a lyre represents music on a Hungarian issue of 1940, to benefit an Artists' Welfare Fund; and stylized musical notes and flowers decorate a Czechoslovakian issue of 1967 promoting a spring music festival.

761. In 1961, for the centenary of her birth, Australia paid a postal tribute to opera singer Dame Nellie Melba (Nellie Porter Mitchell), with a portrait derived from a bust by Sir Bertram MacKennal in the collection of the National Gallery of Victoria, Australia.

762. Violinist, conductor, and composer Eugene Ysaye, who was conductor of the Cincinnati Symphony Orchestra from 1918–22, is pictured on a Belgian issue of 1958, the centenary of his birth.

763. A scene from Franz Lehar's *The Merry Widow*, part of an Austrian series of 1970 on Viennese operettas.

764. Senegal pictured Louis "Satchmo" Armstrong and his horn on a stamp issued in 1971, the year of his death.

764

765

766

767

768

769

765, 766. Ludwig van Beethoven, from a portrait by the nineteenth-century painter Ferdinand Georg Waldmüller, on an Austrian issue. From Mexico, Beethoven's signature and part of the score of his Ninth Symphony. Both stamps were issued in 1970, on the occasion of the 200th anniversary of the birth of the composer.

767. Sweden honored the nineteenth-century Romantic composer Franz Adolf Berwald on the centenary of his death, in 1968, with a stamp showing his profile, his violin, and the opening bar of the overture to his opera *The Queen of Golconda.*

768. The opening bars of the overture to Richard Wagner's *Die Meistersinger von Nürnberg* appear on a German Federal Republic stamp of 1968, the centenary of the first performance of the opera.

769, 770. In 1950, to commemorate the 200th anniversary of the death of Johann Sebastian Bach, the German Federal Republic issued a stamp depicting his seal. West Berlin, honoring the 250th anniversary of the composition of the Brandenburg concertos, in 1971, showed the opening bars of the Second Brandenburg Concerto.

771. A scene from Walter Felsenstein's production of Benjamin Britten's opera based on Shakespeare's *A Midsummer Night's Dream* is presented on this 1973 stamp from the German Democratic

772. Poland represented a piano keyboard on a 1970 stamp honoring the Eighth International Chopin Piano Competition.

773. A design by J. S. Vargas on a Cuban issue of 1972, honoring a children's song competition of the previous year.

774. A lute, from a 1968 Algerian series on musical instruments.

775. A guitarist, from French Polynesia. 1958.

776. In honor of the 150th anniversary of the Alpine Herdsmen's Festival, Switzerland pictured an alphorn, one of the largest of all musical instruments. 1955.

Myths and Legends

777. For Children's Day, 1971, Lebanon issued a stamp showing a scene from the fourteenth-century folktale "The Ravens and Owls." The ravens, who had been defeated in war by the owls, are seen revenging themselves by setting a fire in front of the owls' cave hideaway and destroying them.

778–80. An ancient Chinese folktale, "The Foolish Old Man Who Moved the Mountain," supplied the theme for these 1972 stamps from the People's Republic of China commemorating the new Red Flag Canal. Illustrated are the Taoyuan Aqueduct, the Youth Tunnel, and workers on the cliffs along the canal. The tale is that of a peasant who lived facing a mountain, which prevented him from visiting his friend. He vowed to remove it. Ridiculed by his neighbors, he appealed to the spirits, who caused the mountain to disappear.

778

779

780

783. A wood carving of the ancient Samoan god Tagaloa, who fished Samoa from the sea, from a Western

784

785

784–87. Various mythological figures of the Gulf District, Papua, depicted in 1966 stamps from Papua and New Guinea. These issues were designed by the Reverend H. A. Brown, who served in the Gulf of Papua community for more than a quarter of a century as a pastor of the London Missionary Society.

781. Greek stamp of 1973 showing Mount Olympus, legendary home of the gods.

782. One of a series of stamps issued in 1966–67 by the Himalayan princely state of Bhutan presenting various conceptions of the *Yeti* or "Abominable Snowman."

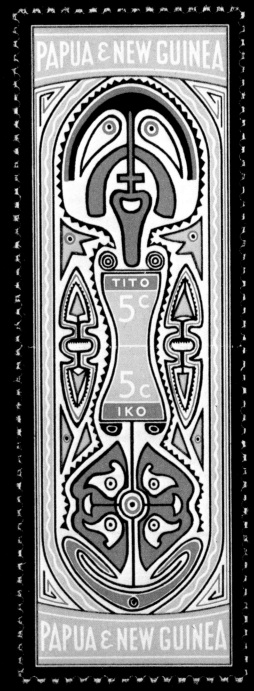

788. From Papua and New Guinea, a depiction of an ancestral memorial board representing the Elema tribe folk heroes Iko and Tito. 1969.

Plants

BAЙKУШEBATA MУPA 1200 Г.-ПИРИН

13st

NR BULGARIA

789. 1,200-year-old pines, from a Bulgarian series on ancient trees. 1964.

790–93. Maple leaves and seeds in the four seasons, from Canada. 1971.

Spring Printemps

Canada 6

790

Summer Été

Canada 6

791

Autumn Automne

Canada 7

792

Winter Hiver

Canada 7

793

794, 795. Cherry blossoms, from a mural in Chishakuin Temple, Kyoto, issued by Japan in 1969 to publicize EXPO '70, held in Tokyo; and cherry blossoms at Yoshinoyama, from a 1970 Japanese issue honoring Yoshino-Kumano National Park.

796

British Honduras

E II R

Epidendrum Cochleatum

The Black Orchid

5c

ORCHIDS OF BELIZE

798

801–3. Maize from Lesotho (1971), raspberries (*Rubus idaeus*) from Romania (1964), and a coffee branch and stylized letter *R*, from Brazil (1957), issued to celebrate the centenary of the founding of Ribeirão Prêto in São Paulo province in 1856.

FLAMBOYANT PLANT

GRENADA 3c

797

796–99. Exotic flowers: the Tussac (*Spartina arundinacea*) from Tristan da Cunha, 1972; the Flamboyant Plant from Grenada, marking Grenada's entry as an Associated State into the British Commonwealth, 1967; a black orchid (*Epidendrum cochleatum*) from British Honduras (now Belize), 1970, and another orchid (*Odontoglossum crispum*) from Colombia, 1947.

800. *Aucoumea klaineana*, from a Gabon series on trees. 1967.

COLOMBIA CORREOS

ODONTOGLOSSUM CRISPUM

5 ORQUÍDEAS COLOMBIANAS CINCO CENTAVOS

AMERICAN BANK NOTE COMPANY.

799

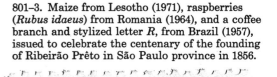

40 BANI

Rubus idaeus L.

POSTA ROMANA

1964   AIDA TASGIAN CONSTANTINESCU

802

OKOUME
AUCOUMEA KLAINEANA   POSTE AÉRIENNE 1967

100 F

REPUBLIQUE GABONAISE

800

LESOTHO

½ CENT

MAIZE

801

BRASIL-CORREIO

cr$2,50

CENTENARIO DE RIBEIRÃO PRETO

SÃO PAULO - 1856-1956

803

226

Portraits

804. King Saul in battle array is shown on this stamp of 1960, part of a New Year's series depicting the kings of Israel.

805

806

808

807

811

805. For the 200th anniversary of Napoleon's birth, St. Lucia portrayed the emperor and Empress Josephine. 1969.

806. George VI, from an Australian series of royal portraits issued 1948–52.

807. Norway commemorated the centenary of the birth of Haakon VII in 1972.

808. Britain's Edward VIII, who abdicated in 1936 to marry an American divorcée, Wallis Simpson, and became Duke of Windsor. 1936.

809. A stylized portrait of Queen Fabiola of Belgium appears on this stamp designed by M. Ianchelevici in honor of the establishment of the Queen Fabiola Foundation for Mental Health. 1970.

809

810. Surinam, an autonomous territory of the Netherlands, portrayed Queen Juliana of the Netherlands on a 1959 stamp.

812

813

814

815

811–15. Portraits of Elizabeth II: from Hong Kong, 1962; from Grenada, a portrait of the queen seated, 1966; from St. Helena, 1959, with the arms of the East India Company, to mark the 300th anniversary of the landing of the company's Capt. John Dutton on St. Helena, May 5, 1659; from Southern Rhodesia, for her coronation, 1953; and an Arnold Machline design, from a British series of 1967–69.

816

817

818

819

816. A Cook Islands stamp issued in 1972 reproduced the 1947 wedding photograph of (then) Princess Elizabeth and Lieut. Philip Mountbatten, Royal Navy. George VI and Queen (Mother) Elizabeth are at the right.

817. Queen Elizabeth II and Prince Philip on their silver wedding anniversary, after a photograph by Norman Parkinson. Great Britain, 1972.

818, 819. For the coronation of Elizabeth II in 1953, New Zealand issued these stamps: a portrait of the queen, and St. Edward's crown and the royal scepter.

820. Queen Salote of Tonga is represented on a heart-shaped stamp issued in 1964 in honor of the Pan-Pacific Southeast Asia Women's Association.

821. Denmark celebrated the wedding of Crown Princess Margrethe to Prince Henrik (Count Henri de Montezat of France) in 1967.

822. Prince Albert of Liège as a youth, on a Belgian stamp of 1938.

823. In 1911 Bavaria commemorated the twenty-fifth anniversary of the regency of Prince Luitpold—a period of great prosperity for the country.

824. Princess Grace of Monaco, on the occasion of the birth of her daughter, Princess Caroline. 1957.

825. Dr. Leo Baeck, chief rabbi of Berlin, was imprisoned by the Nazis at Theresienstadt during World War II. In 1957, on the first anniversary of his death, the German Federal Republic issued a stamp to honor this greatly respected Jewish theologian and spiritual leader.

827. Saint Emerich, known as the saint of youth, is portrayed on a Hungarian stamp of 1930, commemorating the 900th anniversary of the saint's death.

826. A memorial to Pope John XXIII, from Niger. 1965.

828. In 1956 France issued a series of stamps honoring famous men who lived part of their lives in France—Benjamin Franklin among them.

829. From the Commonwealth states of St. Christopher, Nevis, and Anguilla, a portrait of Alexander Hamilton, who was born on the island of Nevis in 1757. 1963.

830. On the 150th anniversary of the birth of Abraham Lincoln, Haiti issued a memorial sheet with four portraits of Lincoln: as a young man, with a log cabin in the background; with the U.S. Capitol; with the Lincoln Memorial; and with the Lincoln Monument. 1959.

828

829

830

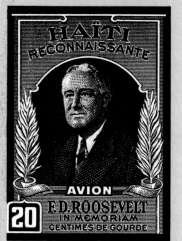

831

831. Franklin D. Roosevelt has been the subject of many stamps; he appears here on a Haitian memorial issue of 1946.

832. From Rwanda, a portrait of John F. Kennedy, on the second anniversary of his assassination. 1965.

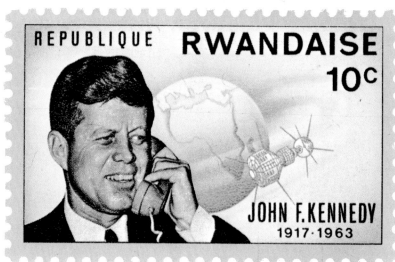

832

833

834

835

836

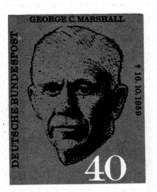

837

839

840

842

843

844

833. Paul Emile Janson, lawyer and statesman, on a Belgian stamp of 1967.

834. To celebrate the twenty-fifth anniversary, in 1970, of the founding of the Second Republic, Austria issued a stamp portraying Leopold Figl, chancellor of the Second Republic from 1945–53.

835. Costa Rican political leader Manuel Aguilar appeared on a stamp honoring the first Congress of Pan-American lawyers in 1961.

836. A memorial to Sir Winston Churchill, from Australia, after the photograph by Yousuf Karsh. 1965.

837. The German Federal Republic paid homage to George Catlett Marshall, the United States secretary of state who, after World War II, joined with President Harry S Truman in establishing an aid-to-Europe program, known as the Marshall Plan. This postal portrait was issued in 1960, commemorating the first anniversary of Marshall's death.

838. Theodor Heuss, first president of the Federal Republic of Germany, on a Saar stamp of 1957. The Saar, under French administration since 1945, became a state in the Federal Republic in 1957.

839. In 1970 Chile honored Paul Harris, the founder of Rotary International, on the centenary of his birth.

840. In 1970 Canada commemorated the 150th anniversary of the birth of Sir Donald Alexander Smith, a Canadian statesman and financier who drove the last spike in Canada's transcontinental railway. Dora de Peterey-Hunt, whose medallion of Hunt is shown, also designed the stamp.

841. In 1959, on the twenty-first anniversary of Kemal Ataturks death, Turkey issued this stamp portraying the Turkish general and statesman.

842. Bulgarian premier Aleksandr Stamboliski was honored on the fiftieth anniversary of his death on a Bulgarian stamp of 1973. The portrait bust is by Andrei Nikolov.

843. Former Chancellor Konrad Adenauer, on a German Federal Republic stamp of 1968.

844. For the fiftieth anniversary, in 1961, of the founding of the Republic of China, the Nationalist Chinese government on Taiwan issued a stamp showing Sun Yat-sen and Chiang K'ai-shek.

845–49. A portrait gallery of revolutionaries, from a Hungarian series of 1919. From left to right: Karl Marx; Alexander Petofi, Hungarian lyric poet and revolutionary; Ignaz Josef Martinovics, Franciscan monk, professor of physics and chemistry, and leader of a republican movement; Gyorgy Dózsa, leader of a peasant revolt against the Hungarian lords; Friedrich Engels.

850. Kevin Barry, an Irish patriot who died in the Irish War of Independence, appeared on an Irish stamp on the fiftieth anniversary of his death. 1970.

851. For the Declaration of Havana, Cuba issued a stamp in 1961 portraying Cuban patriot and revolutionary José Julian Martí.

852. Gandhi, the leader of India's independence struggle, has been represented on stamps from many countries; this one, from Grenada, was issued in 1969 on the centenary of his birth.

850

851

852

853. El Cid Campeador, an eleventh-century soldier and Spanish national hero whose real name was Rodrigo Díaz de Vivar, on a Spanish stamp of 1962, adapted from a 1951 statue by Juan Cristóbal.

МАКСИМ
ГОРЬКИЙ

ЮО ЛЕТ СО ДНЯ РОЖДЕНИЯ

ПОЧТА СССР 1968 4 К

854. For the centenary in 1968
of the birth of Maxim Gorki, the
U.S.S.R. issued this stamp
reproducing V.A. Serov's portrait
of the writer and revolutionist.

855

857

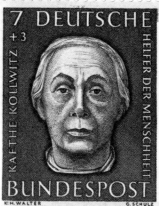

860

858

861

863

862

859

864

865

860. To celebrate the 700th anniversary of the birth of Dante Alighieri, the Vatican in 1965 reproduced a portrait of the poet by Raphael.

861. Kaethe Kollwitz, a painter and lithographer whose pictures of the troubled world of the lower classes spoke for social reform, appeared on a German Federal Republic Welfare Fund stamp in 1954.

862. Marie Curie (Marja Sklodowska Curie), the discoverer of radium and a native of Poland, is portrayed on a Polish stamp in 1967, the centenary of her birth.

863. From the German Democratic Republic, a portrait of composer Günther Ramin. 1957.

864. An Israeli stamp of 1956 honoring Albert Einstein and his theory of relativity, the original manuscript of which is now in the collection of the Hebrew University in Jerusalem.

865. An aborigine appears on a 1950 Australian stamp.

855. Novelist Sidonie Gabrielle Claudine Colette, from a 1973 French series on famous people.

856. Jan Neruda, journalist and short-story writer, from a series honoring Czech writers. Czechoslovakia, 1954.

857. The noted architect Le Corbusier (Charles Édouard Jeanneret), from a Swiss series of stamps portraying famous people. 1972.

858. Werner von Siemens, an engineer and inventor who constructed the first telegraph line in Germany and founded the Siemens electrical industries, is shown on a German Federal Republic stamp of 1966 commemorating the 150th anniversary of his birth.

859. The German Federal Republic in 1955 commemorated the centenary of the birth of Oskar von Miller, an engineer and leader in the electrification of Germany who founded a science museum in Munich.

866. A Grenada issue of 1970 shows the pirate Anne Bonney, who served with "Calico Jack" Rackham.

867. Edward Teach, "Blackbeard," perhaps the most infamous pirate of them all, is depicted on this British Virgin Islands issue. 1970.

866

867

868

869

870

871

868–74. Unlike a portrait in the usual sense of the word, caricature involves distortion or exaggeration of a person's most noticeable facial features. Although intended to poke fun at or satirize someone, caricature can nonetheless be considered a particular type of portraiture, since its effectiveness depends entirely on immediate recognition of the person portrayed.
For a series of UNESCO stamps issued by Czechoslovakia in 1968, Adolf Hoffmeister portrayed cultural personalities of the twentieth century in caricature: American author Ernest Hemingway, Czech playwright Karel Čapek, English dramatist George Bernard Shaw, Russian writer Maxim Gorki, Spanish artist Pablo Picasso, Japanese painter Taikan Koyama, and cinema's bittersweet comic Charlie Chaplin.

872

873

874

Postal History

875

876

877

878

879

880

881

875. Saint Zeno, patron saint of postmen, on a Greek stamp of 1969. Zeno was postmaster under the Roman emperor of the East, Valens, in the fourth century, and later became a hermit.

876. Finland honored the Helsinki Philatelic Exhibition, in 1948, with a stamp showing a postrider.

877, 878. For Stamp Day, 1958, the German Democratic Republic depicted a seventeenth-century post coach. The inauguration of railway-mail service between France and Germany, in 1844, was commemorated a century later with this French stamp showing the first railway-mail car used. 1944.

879. For Stamp Day in 1963, France issued a stamp showing a chariot used to carry mail between Gaul and Rome after Julius Caesar's conquest.

880. Poland celebrated the 400th anniversary of its postal service with a stamp depicting a medieval postman. 1958.

881. Botswana, formerly called Bechuanaland, issued a stamp in 1972 to commemorate the inauguration of a runner post service between Mafeking and Gubulawayo in 1888. The map shows the northern end of the runner's route.

883

884

882. The posthorn, shown on a German Federal Republic stamp of 1952, has been the symbol of postal services from their beginnings.

883, 884. Mechanization of the post office: an Argentinian issue of 1971 picturing Albert Einstein, whose work in phosphorescence mechanics paved the way for developments in electronic postal cancellation; and a Republic of Korea stamp of 1970 showing men using a mail-sorting machine.

885. A United Nations stamp of 1972, designed by Olav S. Mathiesen, represents the passage of a letter from hand to hand.

886

887

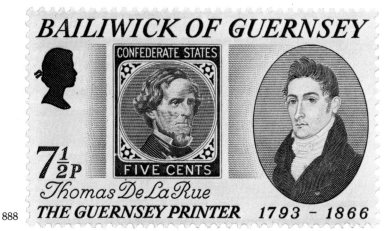

888

889

890

889, 890. Iran, observing the centenary of its postal service in a 1967 series, reproduced the first Persian stamp; Spain displayed its first stamp (1850) on a 1966 issue honoring International Stamp Day.

886–88. Stamps issued to celebrate the anniversary of a country's postal service frequently reproduce actual letters or stamps from an earlier period. Jamaica, commemorating the 300th anniversary of its postal service in 1971, pictured a letter written in 1859; Fiji, celebrating the centenary of its first stamp issue in 1970, showed six stamps ranging in date from 1871 to 1961. In 1971 the Channel island of Guernsey honored a native son, Thomas De La Rue, who was one of the first printers of British stamps, by showing various stamps printed in his lifetime.

891. For a 1971 New York stamp show, Interpex, Western Samoa produced a souvenir sheet showing the New York skyline and a native boat and rowers, as well as reproductions of its first stamp, the 3p Samoa Express stamp of 1877, and one of the first U.S. stamps, the 5c stamp of 1847.

892

892. In 1967 Czechoslovakia issued a series of stamps promoting the World Stamp Exchange, held in Prague in 1968. Some of the series recalled earlier international exhibitions, such as the Sixth International Philatelic Exhibition (SIPEX), held in Washington, D.C., in 1966.

893. For a junior stamp show, Juventus 1969, Luxembourg solicited design ideas from European children and used three designs by Belgian, Austrian, and Swiss children on a souvenir sheet.

893

894. Bulgaria issued a souvenir sheet with four stamps and five promotional labels to mark its Second National Philatelic Exhibition, held in Sofia in 1968.

895. Belgium used the emblem of the Pro-Post Association, which sponsored an international stamp show called Postphila 1967, on a 1967 issue.

895

894

896

900. A United States air-letter sheet of 1971 bearing an imprinted design of birds in flight by Soren Noring.

897

901

901–3. Airmail stamps have inspired a variety of designs depicting planes. A B–17 Flying-Fortress casts a shadow over the pyramids of Giza, from an Egyptian series issued 1959–60; the shadow of a plane appears over the Saar River on a Saar stamp issued in 1948, during the period of French occupation; an early mail plane is depicted flying over Paris on a French stamp of 1936.

898

904

902

899

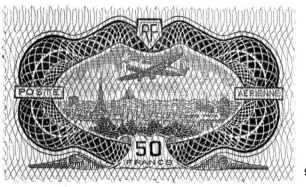

903

905

896–99. United Nations airmail stamps: Olav S. Mathiesen of Denmark (1951), Arne Johnson of Norway (1972), and Ole Hamann of Denmark (1951) used stylized birds as symbols of flight. A 1964 stamp by Hamann shows a winged globe.

904, 905. Two stamps issued by the German Reich in 1944 to celebrate the twenty-fifth anniversary of airmail service: the Lufthansa airline emblem with a Junkers JU–90 seaplane and a Blohm-Voss seaplane.

906

907

906, 907. George Van der Sluis designed these U.S. stamps bearing silhouettes of the delta-wing plane (9c) and a jet airliner (11c) in recognition of the achievements of domestic airmail. 1971.

908. A 1968 United States stamp designed by John Larrecq, to be used for international airmail to Europe and North Africa, suggests a jet in flight. It was reissued in 1971, when the rate was increased to 21 cents.

909. A 1973 stamp from the Channel Island of Jersey presents a pioneer method of airmail: a balloon used to fly letters out of Paris during the siege of 1870, and a letter, posted in Paris on December 29, 1870, and addressed to Jersey, one of the first air letters to reach the island.

910, 911. The Universal Postal Union, which celebrated its centenary in 1974, has been recognized on stamps of numerous countries. The Bern, Switzerland, headquarters of the U.P.U. are pictured on a United Nations stamp of 1971 designed by Olav S. Mathiesen. The statue that stands in front of the headquarters building appears on a Turkish stamp of 1949 issued to commemorate the seventy-fifth anniversary of the U.P.U.

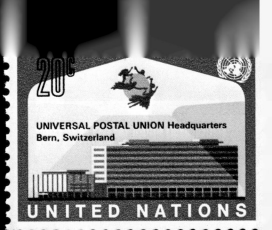

910

911

908

912

912, 913. U.P.U. C Paris in presente over Ile o Sixteenth in 1969, circling t emphasiz contribu

915, 916. Two stamps from the German
Federal Republic, commemorating the 800th
anniversary of the dedication of the Maria Laach
Abbey (1956) and the 1,200th anniversary of the
Benedictine abbey of Ottobeuren (1964).

915   916

Religion

917. A pair of stamps depicting a brass chandelier and ancient Christian symbols,
commemorating the 300th anniversary of the Reformed Church at Paramaribo, Surinam.
1968.

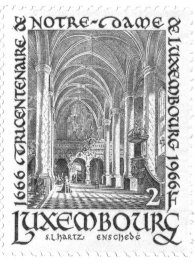

919. The twelfth-century Belgian abbey church
Notre Dame d'Orval was destroyed during the
French Revolution. In 1927 construction of a new
abbey near the ruins was begun. In 1928 Belgium
issued a series of stamps honoring a fund drive
for the project.

918. A painting by Juan Martin depicts
the interior of the former Jesuit church,
now the Cathedral of Luxembourg,
where the Virgin Mary was proclaimed
patron saint in 1666. Luxembourg, 1966.

914. A composite drawing of churches and cathedrals appears on an Italian
stamp honoring the Holy Year of 1950.

Within the stamp:

OREX ISTE TVVS LOCVS EFTERNACA VOCA TS
EXPECTAT VENIA NOCTE DIEQTVA

LUXEMBOURG 150F

COURVOISIER S.A.

920. A Luxembourg stamp with a reproduction of a miniature from the Echternach Cathedral, showing the scriptorium, or manuscript-writing room. 1971.

926. Norway commemorated the 900th anniversary of the Oslo Bishopric in 1971.

927

921. A *garuda* (mythical beast) from the twelfth-century monument of Angkor Thom, Cambodia. The *garuda* is part bird and is considered to be the mount of the Hindu god Vishnu; it is used here on an airmail stamp. 1973.

922. A Buddhist monk receiving alms, on a Laotian stamp of 1957.

922

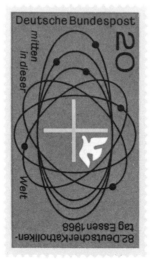

928

923. From Ghana, a symbol representing God's omnipotence. 1959.

924

925

924, 925. The German Federal Republic honored the eighty-second German Catholic Day (1968), and the fifteenth Conference of German Protestant Churches (1973). "Not by Bread Alone" appears on the 1973 stamp.

927, 928. A design by Mrs. Atty Lindenhahn-Rainer depicts one of a number of crosses from the monolithic churches of Lalibela, once capital of Ethiopia, on an Ethiopian stamp of 1967. Ireland used a cross design in its postal tribute to a 1932 International Eucharistic Congress.

FERNANDO POO

2 PTAS

CORREOS

20 LIECHTENSTEIN 930

30 LIECHTENSTEIN 931

70 LIECHTENSTEIN 932

929. Fernando Poo, one of the islands of Spanish Guinea, showed a Madonna on a 1960 issue.

930–32. Christian symbols on a series from Liechtenstein: the Alpha and Omega, the Cross, and XP, the monogram of Christ.

933. A nineteenth-century pewter figure of the Christ Child in a cradle adorns a German Federal Republic Christmas stamp for 1969.

934. A. Palombi's painting *Shipwreck of St. Paul*, in St. Paul's Church, Valetta, Malta, is reproduced on a Maltese stamp of 1960, commemorating the 1,900th anniversary of the saint's shipwreck and landing on Malta.

934

935. *Going to Church in Mora*, a painting by Anders Zorn, from a Swedish tourism series.

936. In an Irish stamp of 1937, St. Patrick, missionary and patron saint of Ireland, invokes a blessing on the Paschal Fire. He is attended by acolytes. The vignette is framed in an outline of the eleventh-century Shrine of St. Patrick's Bell.

247

937–42. A Torah pointer (1966) and five different Torah scrolls (1967), from an Israeli New Year's series.

948. An open book with ornate Hebrew characters was used to commemorate the 400th anniversary of the publication (in 1565) of the *Shulhan Aruk*, a compendium of Jewish religious and civil laws. Israel, 1967.

943–47. The story of Noah and the Ark, as illustrated in an Israeli New Year's series of 1969: "Make yourself an ark of gopher wood" . . . "They went into the ark with Noah two and two" . . . "And the ark floated on the face of the waters" . . . "Then he sent forth a dove" . . . "And the bow is seen in the clouds."

Scenic Views

SINGAPORE $1

View from sea the waterfront in 1861

949. A series of stamps depicting various artists' views of Singapore was issued in 1971; this one, of the waterfront in 1861, is by W. Gray.

955. The Dome of the Rock Mosque and, in the foreground, Absalom's Tomb in the Old City, from an Israeli New Year's series of views of Old and New Jerusalem. 1968.

950. From a Swedish series depicting sites north of the Arctic Circle, a view of the mining town of Kiruna. 1970.

951. A toadstool-shaped rock formation, Romania. 1971.

952. The Saar River near Mettlach, from a pictorial series issued during the period of French occupation. 1947.

954. Street scene in Colonia del Sacramento, the first permanent European settlement (1680) in Uruguay. The stamp was issued in 1970, the 290th anniversary of the settlement.

956. Niedzica Castle, from a Polish tourism issue. 1969.

953. The Devil's Gateway at Baños los Carros, El Salvador. 1969.

800 JAHRE LÜBECK
12+8 12+8
GROSSDEUTSCHES REICH

957

Rothenburg ob der Tauber
DEUTSCHE BUNDESPOST
30
1969

958

900 JAHRE WARTBURG
10+5
DDR

959

5c
DOMINICA

960

LE QUESNOY (Nord)
8F
POSTES
REPUBLIQUE FRANÇAISE

963

CASCADE DE MAN
100F
POSTE AERIENNE
REPUBLIQUE DE CÔTE D'IVOIRE

961

Mauritius
10 CENTS

962

20F
POSTES POINTE DU RAZ FINISTÈRE

964

957–59. Both the German Federal Republic and the German Democratic Republic have used stamps to display sites of historic interest. From West Germany, a view of Lübeck, showing the medieval churches, city gate, and harbor, commemorating the 800th anniversary (1943) of the founding of the city. A 1969 stamp depicting Rothenburg and the Tauber River honors another ancient West German town. And from East Germany, a partial view of Wartburg Castle, where Martin Luther translated the New Testament into German, commemorating the 900th anniversary of the castle. 1966.

960–62. Picturesque views of a waterfall and bird-of-paradise flowers, from Dominica (1971); the Cascade de Man in the Ivory Coast (1970); and a rainbow over a waterfall, from Mauritius (1971).

963, 964. Two French landmarks: the sea at Pointe du Raz, Finistère, from a series issued 1946–48, and the village of Le Quesnoy, built about 1150 and fortified by Charles V in 1527, from a 1957 issue.

965–67. Mountain scenes: from Czechoslovakia, commemorating the twentieth anniversary of Tatra National Park, 1969; of the Val Gardena in Italy's Dolomite Alps, honoring the International Ski Federation (ISF) Tournament, 1970; and, from Nepal, a view of a Gorkha village in the Himalayas.

967

968, 969. Two Austrian forest scenes, both designed by Adalbert Pilch: fir and larch trees, 1962, and stone pines, commemorating a century of university studies of forestry. 1967.

970. The constellation Scorpio, from a series of night sky configurations issued by Botswana. 1972.

970

971

972

973

974

971. For the 1,000th anniversary of the birth of Ibn-al-Haitham, best known as Alhazen, an Arab astronomer and optician considered by some to be the "father of optics," Pakistan issued this stamp in 1969. The diagram, by Ibn-al-Haitham, shows the reflection of light.

972. In 1973 the German Democratic Republic commemorated the 500th anniversary of the birth of Nicolaus Copernicus. At the left side of the stamp is reproduced the title page from his great work, *De Revolutionibus Orbium Coelestium*, in which he established that the earth revolves around the sun.

973, 974. Mathematical equations that have changed the face of the earth are illustrated on these Nicaraguan stamps, from a series of ten issued in 1971. They range from the simple $1 + 1 = 2$ to Einstein's formula $E = mc^2$, which represents the conversion of matter into energy.

253

975

976

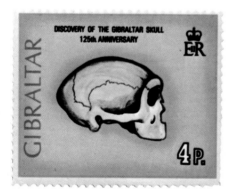

977

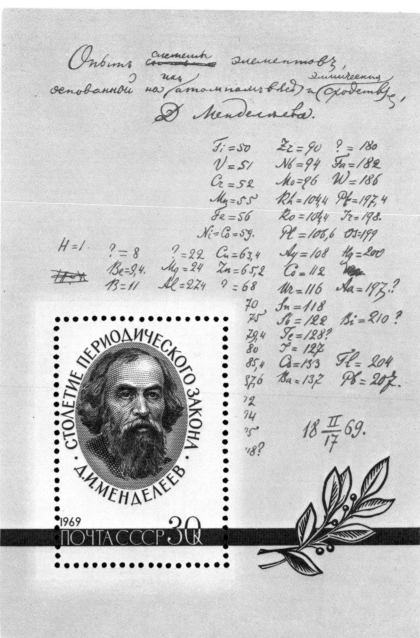

979

975. A comet and galaxy in outer space, as designed by Claude Bottiau for the United Nations, 1963.

976. Ignacy Lukasiewicz, who has been credited with the invention of the kerosene lamp, is pictured on a Polish stamp of 1960 honoring the Fifth Pharmaceutical Science Congress.

977. In 1973 Gibraltar celebrated the 125th anniversary of the discovery of the Gibraltar skull, an relic of Neanderthal man.

978. Greece used an abstract design to symbolize hydrological science, which deals with the distribution, properties, and circulation of water. 1966.

979. Dmitri Ivanovich Mendeleyev was honored by the U.S.S.R. on the centenary of his discovery of the periodic law of elements with a souvenir sheet illustrating his system of classification. 1969.

978

Sports and Games

Many sports events have been pictured on postage stamps. A number of these issues have been occasioned by the quadrennial Olympic Games and similar international competitions. Almost every sport has been represented on stamps at one time or another.

980

983

981

982

984

985

986

987

988

980–88. Field events of the Olympic and other games: The discus thrower, from Bulgaria, honoring the University Games at Sofia, 1961; a right-handed javelin thrower from Finland, for the European Athletic Championships, 1971; a left-handed javelin thrower from Hungary, honoring Angela Nemeth's winning of an Olympic gold medal for javelin, 1969; the pole vault, from French Polynesia, honoring the Second South Pacific Games, 1966; runners on an ancient Greek urn, for the 1964 Olympics in Tokyo; a hurdler from Nigeria, commemorating the 1964 Olympic Games in Tokyo; runners from Great Britain, honoring the Ninth British Commonwealth Games, 1970; and two stamps from a "youth and sport" series from Switzerland, showing sprinters, and girls playing with balls.

989

989, 990. A series of six designs from Cuba spells out the site of the 1972 Olympic Games, while a 1971 stamp from Niger carries the legend "Pre-Olympic Year."

990

991. The German Federal Republic used the Olympic rings to commemorate the 1956 Games in Melbourne.

993

992

992-94. Yachting, as seen by New Caledonia (honoring the One-Ton Boat Races, Auckland, 1971), Portugal (for the 1972 Olympics in Munich), and the Bahamas (from a 1968 series on tourist sports).

994

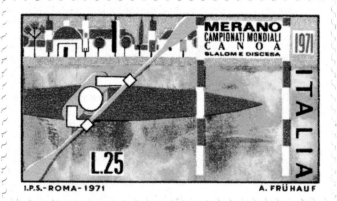

995

996

997

998

999

1000

1001

995, 996. From St. Pierre and Miquelon, a reminder of the world rowing championship contest in Sainte Catherine, 1970, and, from Italy, a similar issue for the world canoeing championship in Merano, 1971.

997, 998. Water-skiing as observed in the Bahamas, 1968, and Lebanon, 1969.

999–1001. A 1973 issue from Singapore commemorating the SEAP (Southeast Asia and Pacific) Games depicts swimmers; divers are shown on a Belgian stamp of 1966; and a Monaco issue honoring the Olympic Games held in London in 1948.

1002

COLOMBIA $1.30 AEREO

VI JUEGOS PANAMERICANOS CALI 1971

DE LA RUE

1003

XVII SVETOVNO PRVENSTVO V GIMNASTIKI

1.25

LJUBLJANA 1970

JUGOSLAVIJA

PTT

XVII SVJETSKO PRVENSTVO U GIMNASTICI

1007. Mongolia has its own "Wild West" and its bucking broncos. 1972.

10 МӨ

МОНГОЛ ШУУДАН

MONGOLIA

1972

1002. Weight-lifting, commemorating the Sixth Pan-American Athletic Games, Cali, Colombia, 1971.

1003. A Yugoslavian issue honoring the Seventeenth World Gymnastics Championship competition, held in Ljubljana in 1970, displays the championship emblem.

7½p

County Cricket 1873-1973

1004

CUBA CORREOS 13

1969

CAMPEONATO MUNDIAL DE BEISBOL AFICIONADO

POSICION FINAL DE LOS EQUIPOS

	Cu	EU	RD	Ve	PR	Col	Nic	Pan	Mex	AH	Gua	G.	P	Ave	Dif.
CUBA	C	1	1	1	1	1	1	1	1	1	1	10	0	1000	—
Estados Unidos	0	U	1	1	1	1	1	1	1	1	1	9	1	900	1
República Dominicana	0	0	B	1	1	1	1	1	S	1	1	7	2	778	2.5
Venezuela	0	0	0	A	1	1	1	1	1	1	1	7	3	700	3
Puerto Rico	0	0	0	0	C	1	0	0	1	1	1	4	6	400	6
Colombia	0	0	0	0	0	A	1	0	1	1	1	4	6	400	6
Nicaragua	0	0	0	0	0	0	M	1	0	1	1	4	6	400	6
Panamá	0	0	0	0	1	1	0	P	0	1	1	4	6	400	6
México	0	0	0	S	0	0	0	1	1	E	0	2	7	222	7.5
Antillas Holandesas	0	0	0	0	0	0	0	0	1	O	S	1	8	111	8.5
Guatemala	0	0	0	0	0	0	0	0	1	S	N	1	8	111	8.5

1005

1004. W. R. Grace, one of England's great cricket players, is remembered in this design by Edward M. Ripley, based on a Harry Furniss drawing. 1973.

1005. Cuba triumphed in the 1969 world baseball championship and provided its own postage-stamp double play—an action scene as well as the box score.

1006. Girls playing field hockey, depicted by L. C. Mitchell on this New Zealand health stamp. 1971.

NEW ZEALAND

3c POSTAGE

1c HEALTH

1006

ARCHIPEL DES COMORES

CHASSE SOUS-MARINE

RF

70F POSTE AERIENNE

CONBET

1008. Underwater fishing off the archipelago of the Comoro Islands. 1972.

HORSE RACING

15c

Bahamas

1009

JOCKEY CLUB BRASILEIRO

BRASIL CORREIO • 1868 1968 • 10 CTS

1010

REPUBLIQUE ISLAMIQUE DE MAURITANIE

15F POSTE AERIENNE

جمهورية الإسلامية الموريتانية

JEUX OLYMPIQUES DE TOKYO-1964

1011

1009–11. Horse racing, from a Bahamas tourism series, 1968; from Brazil, celebrating the centenary of the country's Jockey Club, 1968; and from Mauritania, in honor of the 1964 Olympic Games in Tokyo.

3.50F

ROYAUME DU BURUNDI

IX JEUX OLYMPIQUES D'HIVER · INNSBRUCK

1013

POLSKA

10 GR

JEŹDZIECTWO – UJEŻDŻENIE

B. KAMIŃSKI

PWPW · 67

1012. In the ring: dressage in Poland 1967.

1014   1012   1015

HELVETIA

WELTMEISTERSCHAFTEN DAVOS 1966

5

W. HAETTENSCHWEILER   COURVOISIER S.A.

LESOTHO   12½c

SKIING, MALUTI MOUNTAINS

1013–15. A 1964 Burundi issue honoring the Winter Olympics held that year in Innsbruck; a Swiss stamp of 1965 calling attention to the upcoming World Figure-Skating Championships, held in Davos in 1966; and a 1970 tourism issue from Lesotho depicting skiers in the Maluti Mountains.

1016. The key to track records—a stopwatch, on a Papua and New Guinea stamp issued in honor of the Fourth South Pacific Games, Papeete, 1971.

1016

1017

1017. Boxing, from Guinea, 1963.

1018, 1019. Golf, from a Bahamas tourist issue, 1968, and from the Cook Islands, commemorating the Third South Pacific Games, 1969.

1018

1019

1020

1020–22. In 1967 the German Democratic Republic celebrated its world championship in the biathlon, a contest in which cross-country skiers carrying rifles make stops to shoot at targets set up along a 12.5 mile course. A stamp from a Hungarian hunting-trophies series of 1966 shows, at left, the head of a fallow deer. At right, a tab showing the skeleton of the head bears the place and date of the kill.

1021

1022

1023

1025

1023, 1024. Two world fencing championships occasioned these stamps: from Luxembourg (1954), depicting the foil, épée, saber, mask, and glove; and from Turkey (1970).

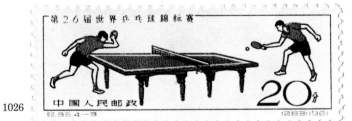

1026

1024

1027

1028

1025. Tennis, anyone? The player is composed of tennis balls on this Czech stamp of 1973, commemorating the eightieth anniversary of lawn tennis in Czechoslovakia.

1026. From the People's Republic of China, a table-tennis match, honoring the world championship match held in Peking in 1961.

1027–29. Cycling has become a worldwide sport. A Belgian issue of 1969 honored the World Cycling Championship held at Zolder, Terlaemen, that year. In 1968 Mali issued a series on early bicycles and automobiles. including this depiction of a Draisienne cycle of 1809. And New Caledonia, on a 1970 issue, showed a map of the island as a background for cyclists, honoring the Fourth New Caledonia Bicycle Tour.

1029

261

1030, 1031. In 1973 France commemorated the fiftieth anniversary of the Le Mans automobile road race. Brazil saluted its star racing driver, Emerson Fittipaldi, with a souvenir sheet that took cognizance of his Grand Prix auto-racing championship in the Formula-1 class in 1972.

1030

1031

4c

surinaamse voetbalbond
1920-1970

SURINAME

1032

4d

World Cup 1966

HARRISON AND SONS LTD

1033

1966 **50F** CHAMPIONNAT MONDIAL DE FOOTBALL

POSTES

REPUBLIQUE DEMOCRATIQUE DU CONGO

1034

DANMARK 60

1035

MEXICO AEREO **80¢**

COPA JULES RIMET 1970

1036

IRAN **14 R.**

FIFTEENTH ASIAN YOUTH FOOTBALL
TOURNAMENT TEHRAN 13-27. APRIL 1973

1037

POSTAGE **3¢** 1967 **1¢** HEALTH

NEW ZEALAND

1038

1032–37. Soccer and football are popular
all over the world, as evidenced by these
stamps. A semiabstract design from
Surinam, representing a soccer field with
the ball in the center, commemorates
the fiftieth anniversary, in 1970, of the
Surinam Soccer Association; action scenes
from Great Britain and the Democratic
Republic of the Congo (now Zaire) honor
the World Cup soccer match in 1966.
A Danish design of 1971 is from a sports
series; a Mexican issue of 1970, in honor
of the Jules Rimet Cup, presents a
whimsical view of a crowd. Iran's 1973
stamp commemorates the Fifteenth
Asian Youth Football Tournament.

1038, 1039. Rugby football, a
forerunner of the American type,
was imported from England into
New Zealand. Two New Zealand
health stamps of 1967 depict
action afield, and preparing for
a kick.

1967 **2½ C**

HEALTH **POSTAGE**

1¢

NEW ZEALAND

1039

1040, 1041. Two stamps issued in 1971 are concerned with a different kind of sport—gambling. Mexico commemorated the 200th anniversary (1970) of its national lottery. The Ivory Coast stamp depicts a gaming table.

1040

1041

1043

1045

1042

1044

1042–45. Chess tournaments have provided the occasion for a number of postage stamps. The Bulgarian issue honored a Balkan Games series in 1947; the French marked the International Chess Festival in Le Havre, in 1966; Iceland's 1972 stamp commemorated the Bobby Fischer–Boris Spassky World Chess Championship, held in Reykjavik in 1972, and Israel in 1964 called attention to the Sixteenth Chess Olympics, held in Tel Aviv.

Symbols

1046. The double-carp insignia, frequently a symbol of the
Republic of China. 1969.

POST DAY 1964

UAR الجمهورية العربية المتحدة

بريد ١٩٦٤

F.I.P EXHIBITION 1866-1966

المعرض الدولي الطوابع العربية المتحدة

M

115+55

١٩٦٦-١٨٦٦ ٥٥+١١٥

1047

ZWANZIG JAHRE

30

Grundgesetz

23. Mai 1949

1919 Weimarer

Verfassung

BUNDESREPUBLIK
DEUTSCHLAND

1969

1048

DEUTSCHE BUNDES POST 10+5

DEUTSCHES MUSEUM

50 JAHRE

1049

3d

1ST ANNIVERSARY CASABLANCA CONFERENCE

JAN. 4, 1962

GHANA

1051

UNITED STATES POSTAL SERVICE

U.S.MAIL

8 cents

1052

LUFTHANSA 1955

DEUTSCHE

20

DEUTSCHE BUNDESPOST

1050

INTERNATIONAL CIVIL AVIATION ORGANIZATION · ORGANISATION DE L'AVIATION CIVILE INTERNATIONALE

1945   1955

5¢

CANADA
POSTES · POSTAGE

ΣΥΝΕΔΡΙΟΝ "ΑΗΕΡΑ" 1970

ΕΛΛΑΣ-HELLAS   ΔΡ. 6

1047. The arms of the United Arab Republic appear above the Egyptian pyramids on a 1964 stamp issued for Post Day.

1048. To celebrate the twentieth anniversary of the founding of the German Federal Republic, which came into being in 1949, after Hitler's defeat, the Bonn government issued a stamp showing the emblems of both the Weimar Republic of 1919 and the Federal Republic.

1055

1056

1049. The seal of the German Museum of Science and Technology, an owl and a cogwheel, was used by the German Federal Republic for a stamp commemorating the museum's fiftieth anniversary. 1953.

1050. The trademark of Lufthansa, the German airline, appears on a stamp issued by the German Federal Republic when the airline resumed service in 1955.

1051. Ghana's flag, a map of Africa, and a dove are used as symbols celebrating the first anniversary of the Casablanca Conference of African heads of state. 1962.

1052. In 1971 the United States Post Office Department was reorganized and became the quasi-governmental United States Postal Service. The service adopted this insignia, designed by Loewy-Snaith, Inc., New York.

1053. In 1955 Canada observed the tenth anniversary of the International Civil Aviation Organization, the only United Nations agency headquartered in the country.

1054. The American Hellenic Educational Progressive Association held its 1970 congress in Athens; a Greek stamp honoring the congress includes maps of Greece and the Western Hemisphere and the AHEPA emblem.

1055–58. Marianne, used as a symbol of France on numerous stamps, as imagined by Edmond Dulac (1944), Jean Cocteau (1961), and Pierre Gandon (1945). Another much-used symbol is the Gallic cock; the version shown here is by Albert Decaris, 1962.

1057

1058

1059

1060

1061

1062

1063

1064

1059–64. The abbey church of Notre Dame d'Orval was destroyed during the French Revolution. In 1927 a new abbey was begun near the ruins. Funds were obtained, in part, from the sale of postage stamps with an added denomination, such as these, issued in 1943, whose intricate letters were used both together and individually.

1065

1066

1067

1065–68. The seals of four British colonies, as depicted on their stamps: Grenada (1966), St. Lucia (1949–50), Trinidad and Tobago (1964), and the British Virgin Islands (1947). George VI is also portrayed on the Virgin Islands issue.

1068

1069. Stamp issued in 1946 to commemorate the founding of the Hungarian People's Republic.

1070. Symbols of immigration (the ship), assimilation (factories) and settlement (houses) make up an Israeli stamp commemorating the fiftieth anniversary of the founding of Keren Hayesod, an international group seeking to implement the World War I Balfour Declaration and establish a Jewish homeland. 1970.

1071. A geometric design spells out EUROPA on a Finnish stamp honoring the European Security and Cooperation Conference, held in Helsinki, 1973.

1074, 1075. Belgian stamps commemorating the festivals of Flanders and Wallonia. 1971.

1074

1072

1072, 1073. The worldwide civic organization Lions International was honored with stamps by the Cameroons (1970) and Luxembourg (1967), the latter stamp commemorating the organization's fiftieth anniversary.

1073

1075

1076

1077

1076–81. A great variety of designs and symbols have been used to popularize trade fairs. Belgium honored the Ghent Fair in 1970; Brazil paid tribute to the French industrial fair Franca '71; the German Federal Republic advertised the 1925 Trade Exposition in Munich; the German Democratic Republic, the 1959 Leipzig Fair. India used a hand to symbolize cooperation for the Third Asian International Trade Fair in 1972. Malta noted the Tenth Malta Trade Fair in 1966.

1082. In 1963 Burundi celebrated the first anniversary of its entry into the United Nations with a stamp displaying the arms of the country with those of the U.N. and the Food and Agriculture Organization.

1078

079

1085

1084

U.S. POSTAGE 8c

AMERICAN
REVOLUTION
BICENTENNIAL
1776-1976

1083. Uruguay paid its respects
to the Asociación Latino
Americana de Libre Comercio
(ALALC), the Latin American
free-trade association, with a
stamp urging "A common effort
for a better destiny." 1970.

1084, 1085. In 1965, to commemorate both International Cooperation Year and
its own twentieth anniversary, the United Nations used this design by
Olav S. Mathiesen, as did a number of nations. In 1966 the U.N. used another
Mathiesen design to honor the World Federation of United Nations Associations.

1086. The insignia of the American
Revolution Bicentennial Commission
(now, Administration), designed by
Chermayeff & Geismar Associates, New
York, on a stamp issued July 4, 1971,
as the United States began to prepare
for its Bicentennial celebration.

Organizzazione
Internazionale
del Lavoro 1919-1969

POSTE ITALIANE L. 90

I.P.S. - ROMA 1969

1088

REPUBLIQUE FRANÇAISE

0.90

GRAND ORIENT DE FRANCE 1773-1973

1090

1090. France observed the 200th anniversary
of the Grand Orient (Free Masons) of France
in 1973.

1089

5c   AUSTRALIA

INTERNATIONAL LABOUR ORGANISATION 1919-1969
GEORGE HAMORI   RBA

1087

1087–89. Organized labor, too, has been the subject of stamps.
In 1970 Israel marked the fiftieth anniversary of
Histadrut, its general federation of labor; in 1969 Italy and
Australia commemorated the fiftieth anniversary of the
International Labor Organization.

271

1091. To commemorate the fiftieth anniversary of the International Automobile Show, in 1971, Belgium issued a design of a car formed by the letters "auto."

1092. The Republic of Tunisia in 1973 commemorated a Pan-Arab auto rally with a design showing a racing car in the form of the Arab crescent.

Transportation

1093. In 1959 Hungary issued a stamp series to publicize the national Museum of Transportation; this Czonka car is from the series.

1094. A Daimler automobile. c. 1910, from a 1969 series on antique cars issued by the Republic of the Niger.

1095–97. A locomotive of 1835, from a 1960 German Federal Republic issue commemorating the 125th anniversary of German railroads; from Hungary, an old locomotive, one of a 1959 stamp series issued to publicize the national Museum of Transportation; and, from Malawi, a 1968 issue showing a Diesel railcar of 1955 vintage.

1096

1095

1097

1098

1098. To commemorate EXPO '67 in Montreal, Romania issued a design showing a string of cars on a monorail leaving the United States Pavilion at the exposition.

1099. Mexican stamp of 1969 marking the opening that year of Mexico City's subway system.

1100. A funicular railway, one of a series issued by the British colony of Gibraltar in 1967 to commemorate International Tourist Year.

1099

1100

1101. A bridge of creeping vines at Lieupleu is depicted on a 1965 stamp issued by the Republic of the Ivory Coast.

1104. Japan in 1962 commemorated the opening of the Wakoto suspension bridge in northern Kyushu.

1105. A bridge made of liana from the Federal Republic of Cameroon. 1971.

1106. The beach at Rio de Janeiro, Brazil, Sugarloaf Mountain, and a modern highway, honoring the Eleventh International Highway Congress. 1959.

1102. One of the many Danube bridges, the Giurgeni Bridge, from Romania, 1972.

1103. The British crown colony of Hong Kong in 1972 issued a stamp to mark the inauguration of the four-lane Cross Harbour Tunnel linking the island with Kowloon on the mainland.

1107. The plan of the H.M.S. *Bounty*, on a Pitcairn Islands stamp of 1969. In a mutiny led by Fletcher Christian, William Bligh, the ship's master, and nonmutinying crewmen were cast adrift in an open boat, in which they sailed 4,000 miles to safety. Christian and his fellow mutineers settled on Pitcairn Island after the *Bounty* foundered there.

274

HMS BLANCHE

TURKS & CAICOS ISLANDS

Vessels

5 CENTS

E II R

1108. From the Turks and Caicos Islands, an old sailing vessel, the H.M.S. *Blanche*. 1973.

2d

FALKLAND ISLANDS

The Great Britain 1843

1109

4d

Falkland Islands

The Great Britain 1845

1110

1109–13. A 1970 series from the British colony of Falkland Islands presents the life and death of a great ship—the *Great Britain*—with views of the ship in 1843, 1845, 1876, 1886, and 1970.

9d

Falkland Islands

The Great Britain 1876

1112

1/-

Falkland Islands

The Great Britain 1886

1111

2/-

Falkland Islands

The Great Britain 1970

1113

1114. The German Democratic Republic commemorated the construction of a port at Rostock with a view of Rostock harbor and Rostock's landmark, the seven towers. The German inscription reads "The Baltic—Sea of Peace." 1958.

20 DEUTSCHE DEMOKRATISCHE REPUBLIK

OSTSEE·MEER DES FRIEDENS

O·SEEHAFEN ROSTOCK

1114

VITO DUMAS
"EL MAS GRANDE NAVEGANTE SOLITARIO..." (SLOCUM ASSOC.)

68 PESOS

AEREO

R. ARGENTINA

CASA DE MONEDA   "VI-1968"   A. BOERO D·6

1115

1115, 1116. Argentina and Great Britain paid tribute to men who sailed around the world alone. The Argentinian stamp, issued in 1968, honors Vito Dumas, who made his voyage on the *Legh II* in 1943. Britain in 1967 commemorated the voyage of Francis Chichester in 1966–67 aboard the *Gipsy Moth IV*. The tiny figure before the mast represents Sir Francis (he was later knighted for his voyage).

142

GIPSY MOTH IV
GOAMAN

1/9

HARRISON

1116

UNITED SOCIETY FOR THE PROPAGATION OF THE GOSPEL

'Ye shall be witnesses unto Me...
unto the uttermost parts of the earth – Jesus'

TRISTAN DA CUNHA

4d

1117. A nineteenth-century sailing ship off the coast of Tristan da Cunha, in a 1969 stamp honoring the United Society for the Propagation of the Gospel.

5C MACQUARIE LIGHTHOUSE 1818

AUSTRALIA

1118. To celebrate the 150th anniversary of its first lighthouse, the Macquarie Tower, Australia in 1968 reproduced a drawing of the original lighthouse.

1119

The United Nations, which began issuing its own stamps in 1951, has used them to promote the universal goals of peace, justice, and unity.

1119, 1120. Two renditions of the U.N.'s headquarters building —a 1951 design by Leon Helguera and a 1968 design by Olav S. Mathiesen.

United Nations

1120

1121

UNITED NATIONS 聯合國
NACIONES UNIDAS
NATIONS UNIES
1C
ОБЪЕДИНЕННЫЕ НАЦИИ

1121–24. O. C. Meronti in a 1951 U.N. first issue pictured the people of the world viewing a radiant sun, represented by the U.N. wreath symbol. Claude Bottiau provided the design for the tenth anniversary of the U.N. Charter, 1955, Olav S. Mathiesen's airmail design was used for a 1968 postal card; Herbert M. Sanborn in 1961 showed flags of the nations of the world with a quote from the preamble to the charter.

1122

TENTH ANNIVERSARY
DECIMO ANIVERSARIO
DIXIEME ANNIVERSAIRE
CHARTER OF THE UNITED NATIONS
We the peoples of the United Nations...
3c
ДЕСЯТАЯ ГОДОВЩИНА 十週年紀念

1123

UNITED NATIONS ОБЪЕДИНЕННЫЕ НАЦИИ
13C AIR MAIL
NATIONS UNIES 聯合國 NACIONES UNIDAS

1124

NATIONS UNIES 聯合國
UNITED NATIONS
To unite our strength
NACIONES UNIDAS
30c
ОБЪЕДИНЕННЫЕ НАЦИИ

1125

NACIONES UNIDAS 聯合國 NATIONS UNIES
60c
UNITED NATIONS ОБЪЕДИНЕННЫЕ НАЦИИ

1126

UNITED NATIONS 聯合國
NACIONES UNIDAS
NATIONS UNIES
11c
ОБЪЕДИНЕННЫЕ НАЦИИ

1127

UNITED NATIONS
NACIONES UNIDAS
ОБЪЕДИНЕННЫЕ НАЦИИ
UN
聯合國 NACIONES UNIDAS
13c
NATIONS UNIES

1125–29. Stamps incorporating United Nations symbols, designed by Robert Perrot (60c, 1971); Olav S. Mathiesen (11c, 1962); Leszek Holdanowicz and Marek Freudenreich (13c, 1969); Ole Hamann ($1.00, 1966); and Herbert M. Sanborn (4c, 1958).

1128

$1
UNITED NATIONS

1129

NACIONES UNIDAS 聯合國 NATIONS UNIES
ОБЪЕДИНЕННЫЕ НАЦИИ UNITED NATIONS
4c

1130

1131

1130, 1131. U.N. stamps often cite specialized agencies and their work. Ole Hamann created a symbolic pattern of agricultural, industrial, and trade symbols to honor the Economic Commission for Europe (1959); Olav S. Mathiesen captured the idea of the U.N. aims for housing and community programs (1962).

1132–34. Stalks of wheat have been a much-used symbol in the U.N.'s global fight against hunger. A Dirk van Gelder design of a single wheat stalk honored the U.N. Food and Agriculture Organization (1954). The U.N.'s Freedom from Hunger campaign, initiated in 1963, elicited stamp designs from dozens of nations as well as from the U.N. itself; two are shown, from the U.N. (designed by Ole Hamann) and from the tiny principality of Dubai.

1135. The U.N. seal and the German eagle are portrayed in a stamp designed by Karl Blase, marking the German Federal Republic's entry into the U.N. in 1973.

1132

1133

1134

1135

1136

1136. A stylized globe and weathervane was designed by Hatim Elmekki of Tunisia for a 1964 U.N. issue; it was also used for an envelope stamp.

1137, 1138. For its twenty-fifth anniversary, in 1970, the U. motto was "Peace, Justice and Progress," a theme appearin on its stamps and medals. A stamp with "Justice" mistaker omitted was printed; it was replaced by a new issue that included all three words. The stamp was designed by Ole Hamann.

1139. Renato Ferrini, designer of this U.N. stamp of 1962 visualized the light from the earth illuminating hands holding the letters "UN," symbolizing the unity of the w peoples.

1140

1141

1142

1143

1144

1146

1145

1147

1148

1149

1150

1151

1152

1140-52. Stamps commemorating the role of the U.N. have been issued by many of its member nations. The United States, Tunisia, Sweden, Senegal, Canada, Mali, Malaysia, Japan, Guyana, and Denmark were among the nations that issued stamps to commemorate the twenty-fifth anniversary of the world organization in 1970. Tunisia honored U.N. Day in 1962 and Iran, U.N. Stamp Day in 1967. Mexico commemorated the twenty-fifth anniversary of the United Nations Educational, Scientific, and Cultural Organization (UNESCO) in 1971.

Unusual Reproduction

1155

1153

1154

1153–55. The Himalayan nation of Bhutan utilized unusual techniques of reproduction for a number of its stamps, including a three-dimensional portrayal of an American astronaut on the moon (1972); an embossed lithograph of Degas's painting *The Dancing Lesson* (1972); and a portrait of John F. Kennedy embossed on plastic (1972).

1156. Of all things, Bhutan in 1973 came up with "talking stamps"—actual records. How well they played after cancellation may be questioned. An example of gimmickry at its worst.

1156

War and Peace

NAPOLEON · AFTER A PAINTING BY DAVID
AND NAPOLEON'S TOMB ON ST. HELENA

150th ANNIVERSARY OF THE DEATH OF NAPOLEON 1821

St. HELENA 2ᵖ

1157. St. Helena commemorated the 150th anniversary of the death of Napoleon, showing his tomb under trees on St. Helena. Reproduced in the background is a painting by Jacques-Louis David, *Napoleon Crossing the Alps*.

1158

1159

1160

1158–60. Malta has been a strategic point in Mediterranean struggles from the time of the Punic Wars between Rome and Carthage. The 1p stamp (1965) shows a broken pillar bearing inscriptions on those wars. The Turks, who unsuccessfully besieged the island for many years, were resisted by the Knights of Malta, led by Jean Parisot de la Valette, for whom Malta's capital, Valletta, is named. A 1965 stamp commemorating the 400th anniversary of the beginning of the siege depicts the Turkish fleet. A 1968 issue honoring the 400th anniversary of the death of La Valette shows his tomb in the Church of St. John, Valletta.

1161. Poland in 1960 recalled the defeat in 1410 of the Teutonic Knights by Polish and Lithuanian troops at Grünwald (known today as Tannenberg).

1162. This Hungarian stamp of 1952, issued to publicize Army Day, September 20, pays homage to Ilona Zrinyi, wife of the seventeenth-century prince of Transylvania, Francis I Rákóczi, who, with Ilona's father, Peter Zrinyi, entered into an unsuccessful conspiracy against Emperor Leopold I, the king of Bohemia and Hungary.

1163. The 400th anniversary of the Battle of Lepanto (October 7, 1571), in which a combined Spanish, Papal, and Venetian fleet crushed a Turkish fleet, is commemorated in this stamp from Spain. 1971.

1164. Argentinian stamp depicting a Spanish conquistador and sword, marking the 400th anniversary of the founding of the city of Jujuy. 1961.

1165. Adam Dollard des Ormeaux, a French explorer and commandant of the garrison at Montreal, in 1660 led a small expeditionary force up the Ottawa River in an attempt to save the city from the Iroquois. At Long Sault Rapids he fought a week-long battle against a large Iroquois band, He and his companions were killed in this battle, whose 300th anniversary is marked by this Canadian stamp of 1960.

1161

1162

1163

1165

1164

1166. In 1970, for the twenty-fifth anniversary of the Potsdam Agreement (1945) the German Democratic Republic issued a stamp adapted from a photograph of the participants at the conference table. They are (1) Vyacheslav M. Molotov, Soviet foreign minister; (2) Premier Joseph Stalin; (3) Andrei A. Gromyko, then Soviet ambassador to the United States; (4) James F. Byrnes, U.S. secretary of state; (5) President Harry S Truman; (6) Prime Minister Clement Attlee of Britain, who replaced Winston Churchill after the latter's political defeat; (7) Ernest Bevin, British foreign secretary. The parley established Allied control over Germany after her defeat in World War II.

(1)   (2)   (3)   (4)   (5)

UNTERZEICHNUNG DES

POTSDAMER ABKOMMENS

2.8.1945 · 25. JAHRESTAG DER

25 JAHRE POTSDAMER ABKOMMEN

25 DDR

10 DDR

UNTERZEICHNUNG DES

ПОТСДАМСКОЕ СОГЛАШЕНИЕ
POTSDAM AGREEMENT
LES ACCORDS DE POTSDAM
POTSDAMER ABKOMMEN

2.8.1945-25 JAHRESTAG DER

POTSDAMER ABKOMMENS

20 DDR

1166

(6)   (7)

1167. For the fortieth anniversary of the World War I armistice, in 1958, France recalled her soldiers who died in that war.

REPUBLIQUE FRANÇAISE

POSTES 15F

40ème ANNIVERSAIRE DE L'ARMISTICE

1167

REPUBLIQUE · FRANÇAISE

A TOUS LES FRANÇAIS
La France a perdu une bataille!
Mais la France n'a pas perdu la guerre!

Des gouvernements de rencontre ont pu capituler, cédant à la panique, oubliant l'honneur, livrant le pays à la servitude. Cependant, rien n'est perdu!

Rien n'est perdu, parce que cette guerre est une guerre mondiale. Dans l'univers libre, des forces immenses n'ont pas encore donné. Un jour, ces forces écraseront l'ennemi. Il faut que la France, ce jour-là, soit présente à la victoire. Alors, elle retrouvera sa liberté et sa grandeur. Tel est mon but, mon seul but!

Voilà pourquoi je convie tous les Français, où qu'ils se trouvent, à s'unir à moi dans l'action, dans le sacrifice et dans l'espérance.

Notre patrie est en péril de mort. Luttons tous pour la sauver!

VIVE LA FRANCE !

GÉNÉRAL DE GAULLE
QUARTIER-GÉNÉRAL,
4, CARLTON GARDENS,
JUIN 1940   LONDON, S.W.1.

0,25 +0,05 POSTES

1964-XXe ANNIVERSAIRE DE LA LIBERATION

1168. Charles de Gaulle, as leader of the Free French during World War II, used posters to appeal for aid. One of these was adapted for a French stamp of 1964, commemorating the twentieth anniversary of the liberation of France.

US ARMY   US POSTAGE   3c

1169. The six planes shown flying over the Arch of Triumph and the Champs Elysées as American troops paraded on August 29, 1944, were B–29 bombers—never used in Europe in World War II. For this 1945 United States stamp, they were superimposed on a photograph by Peter J. Carroll of the Associated Press, at the suggestion of Gen. George C. Marshall, chief of staff, U.S. Army. The parade, which honored the role of American troops in the liberation of France, was, literally, the line of march of the troops to the front lines.

DU VERCORS

A LA MEMOIRE DES RESISTANTS

REPUBLIQUE FRANÇAISE

GILIOLI

POSTES   0,30

1170

1942 1967

3/-

Malta

1171

Gefangenen

Gedenket unserer

DEUTSCHE BUNDESPOST

10

1172

1170-72 France in 1962 memorialized her resistance at Vercors in World War II; Malta, awarded the George Cross for gallantry in World War II, issued a stamp in 1967 to commemorate the twenty-fifth anniversary of the event; and a German Federal Republic stamp of 1953 reads "Remember our prisoners of war."

285

1173

1174

1175

1173. After World War II the Allied Military Government operated the mails in occupied areas of Europe. This A.M.G. overprint for Trieste appears on a 1947 Italian stamp commemorating the fiftieth anniversary of radio.

1174. Below a representation of the Leyte Landing Monument, an outline drawing depicts Gen. Douglas MacArthur leading his aides ashore at Leyte, October 20, 1944, in a Philippine stamp issued for the twenty-fifth anniversary of the landing. 1969.

1175. Victor S. McCloskey, Jr., designed this 1945 United States stamp memorializing U.S. Marines raising the American flag on Mt. Suribachi on the island of Iwo Jima that year. The design is from a photograph made by Joe Rosenthal of the Associated Press.

1176

1177

1176, 1177. The dove, proverbial symbol of peace, is depicted on a Turkish issue of 1969 marking the twentieth anniversary of the North Atlantic Treaty Organization, and an Egyptian stamp of 1957 for an Afro-Asian People's Conference in Cairo.

1178

1179

The defeat of Hitler in World War II brought a flood of liberation issues.

1178, 1179. Belgium and the Netherlands used the "V" as a symbol of victory, Belgium in 1944 and the Netherlands in 1970, celebrating the twenty-fifth anniversary of liberation.

1180. Albania celebrated the twentieth anniversary of its liberation and the establishment of the People's Republic, in 1964.

1181. In 1970 France commemorated the twenty-fifth anniversary of the liberation of the German concentration camps.

1180

1181

1184

1185

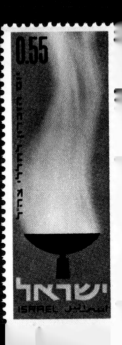

1190

1191

1190–92. A pair of Soviet issues commemorating the
twenty-fifth anniversary of the liberation of Hungary and
Czechoslovakia: the Hungarian coat of arms and Budapest, and
the arms of the Czechoslovak Socialist Republic and Prague.
Poland, celebrating the twenty-fifth anniversary of the
liberation of Warsaw, depicted a statue of Nike, goddess
of victory, and the Polish flag on its 1970 issue.

1193. Evgeny Vuchetich's *Beating Swords into Ploughshares*, presented by the U.S.S.R.
to the United Nations on December 4, 1959, is pictured on a Russian stamp of 1970.

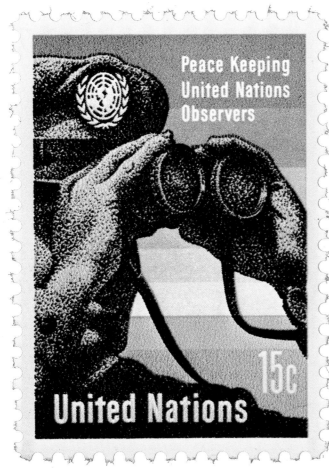

1197, 1198. The peaceful use of outer space is advocated in a 1962 U.N. stamp designed by Kurt Plowitz, and the peaceful use of the sea-bed, in a 1972 U.N. issue designed by P. Rahikainen of Finland.

1197

1198

1199

1199. This U.N. stamp designed by Arne Johnson of Norway urges the nonproliferation of nuclear weapons. 1972.

1200. The Australian Antarctic Territory commemorated the tenth anniversary of the Antarctic Treaty, which reserved the continent for peaceful purposes, with this view of sastrugi, or ridges of snow formed by the action of the wind. 1971.

1194. The peace-keeping function of the U.N. is reflected on a number of stamps; a U.N. military observer was portrayed by Ole Hamann for a 1966 stamp issued by the organization.

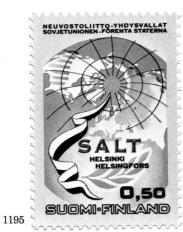

1195

1196

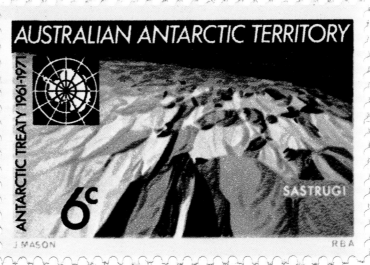

1200

1195, 1196. The Strategic Arms Limitation Talks between the United States and the U.S.S.R. began in Finland in 1970 and concluded with the signing of a treaty in Moscow in May 1972. Two stamps from Finland, one from 1970 and one from 1972, mark the opening and termination of the talks.

Weather and Natural Phenomena

1201

1202

1203

1201–3. The weather, too, has found its way onto stamps.
To commemorate the centenary of the World Meteorological
Organization in 1973, the Netherlands offered a rainbow; the
African nation of Botswana turned to Scandinavian mythology
for its depiction of the Frost Giant, Ymir; and Sweden presented
a view of the earth as seen from a U.N. satellite.

1204. United Nations issue of 1972 showing a lovely cloudy sky.

1205

1206

1205–7. Solar eclipses as seen from Manuae Island, in the Cook Islands, in 1965, and from Mauritania and Senegal in 1973—the Mauritanian issue stressing scientific observation, the Senegalese depicting the successive phases of the eclipse.

1207

1208. The People's Republic of China paid tribute to Chinese meteorology in 1958 with a drawing of a weathercock.

1209. Tunisia, honoring World Meteorological Day in 1964, took note of an "unsettled forecast."

1210. A volcano erupting on an island in Taal Lake, Luzon, the Philippines. 1965.

Bibliography

Books and Periodical Articles

Bloss, Roy S. *Pony Express. The Great Gamble*. Berkeley, Calif.: Howell-North, 1959.

Diringer, David. *The Alphabet*. New York: Philosophical Library, 1948.

Fricke, Charles. *Centennial Handbook of the First Issue U.S. Postal Card*. 2 vols. Bellair, Fla.: United Postal Stationery Society, 1973.

Friedman, Herbert A. "Allied Forgeries of the Postage Stamps of Nazi Germany." *American Philatelist*, February 1971.

————. "British Espionage Forgeries of the First World War." *American Philatelist*, September 1973.

————. "German Wartime Parodies of British Stamps." *Journal of the Society of Philatelic Americans*, February 1974.

Garber, Paul. *50th Anniversary of U.S. Airmail, 1918–1968*: Washington, D.C.: Airlines Postal Affairs Committee and the Air Transport Association of America, 1968.

Gelb, Ignace J. *A Study of Writing*. Chicago: University of Chicago Press, 1963.

Gentleman, David. *Design in Miniature*. London: Studio Vista Blue Star House, 1972.

Gibbon, Edward. *The History of the Decline and Fall of the Roman Empire*. New York: Modern Library, 1932.

Grant, Campbell. *Rock Art of the American Indian*. New York: Thomas Y. Crowell Co., 1967.

Harlow, Alvin F. *Paper Chase: The Amenities of Stamp Collecting*. New York: Henry Holt & Co., 1940.

————. *Old Post Bags*. New York: D. Appleton, 1928.

Herodotus. *The Persian Wars*. Translated by George Rawlinson. New York: Modern Library, 1942.

Horowicz, Kay, and Lowe, Robson. *The Colonial Posts of the United States of America, 1606–1783*. London: Robson Lowe Ltd., 1967.

Hurt, E. F. *Thurn und Taxis. Founders of the Posts of Europe*. Vol. 8. Jamaica, N.Y.: Billig Handbook, 1948.

Loeb, Julius. "The Pony Express." *American Philatelist*. November 1930.

Lowe, Robson. *The British Postage Stamp of the Nineteenth Century*. London: National Postal Museum, 1968.

————. *The Encyclopedia of British Postage Stamps*. 2 vols. London: Robson Lowe Ltd., 1935–36 (and later eds.).

Mason, William. *A History of the Art of Writing*. New York: Macmillan Co., 1920.

Nathan, M. R., and Boggs, W. S. *The Pony Express*. New York: Collectors Club, 1962.

Ogg, Oscar. *An Alphabet Source Book*. New York: Harper & Bros., 1940.

Perry, Elliott. *The First United States Postage Stamp*. Portland, Me.: Severn-Wylie-Jewett Co., 1920.

Perry, Elliott, and Hall, Arthur G. *100 Years Ago, February-1842-August, Centenary of the First Adhesive Postage Stamp in the United States*. State College, Pa.: American Philatelic Society, 1942.

Piendl, Max. *Thurn und Taxis, 1517–1867*. Frankfurt: Bund Deutscher Philatelisten e. V., 1967.

Polo, Marco. *The Travels of Marco Polo*. Translated by R. E. Latham. Baltimore, Md.: Penguin Books, 1958.

Rider, John F. "Some Observations on the Postal History of the Republic of Venice." *Postal History Journal* (1966–68; seven installments).

Robinson, Howard. *The British Post Office, a History*. Princeton, N.J.: Princeton University Press, 1948.

Russo, Anthony C. "Sardinian Letter Sheets." *Philately,* August 12, 1946.

Scheele, Carl H. *A Short History of the Mail Service*. Washington: Smithsonian Institution Press, 1970.

Schriber, Les, Sr. *Encyclopedia of Designs, Designers, Engravers, Artists of United States Postage Stamps, 1847–1900*. State College, Pa.: American Philatelic Society, 1962.

Staff, Frank W. *The Penny Post, 1680–1918*. London: Lutterworth Press, 1964.

Todd, T. *William Dockwra and the Rest of the Undertakers, the Story of the London Post, 1680–82*. Edinburgh: C. J. Cousland & Sons Ltd., 1952.

Woodward, A. M. Tracey. *The Postage Stamps of Japan and Dependencies*. London: Harris Publications, Ltd. 1928.

CATALOGS

Minkus New 1975 World Wide Stamp Catalog. New York: Minkus Publications, 1975.

Scott Standard Postage Stamp Catalogue, 1975. New York and Omaha: Scott Publishing Co., 1975.

Stanley Gibbons Stamp Catalogue. London: Stanley Gibbons Ltd., 1973.

Index

302